Positioned for Power

The Working Woman's Guide to Thriving in Life

ANGELINE LAWRENCE

ISBN 10: 0-692-53409-1
ISBN 13: 978-0-692-53409-0

Printed in USA

Dedication

This book is dedicated to my beautiful husband and children. I especially want to thank my mother and grandmother who taught me the power of prayer at a young age.

Table of Contents

Foreword

Workplace bullying is a serious problem for women in America. As a former target, Christ led me to deal with my perpetrators using a different approach. He did not lead me to contact the EEOC (Equal Employment Opportunity Commission) or a lawyer. Rather, I focused on rebuilding my spirit and worked to grow as a Christian. The question became, "How can I combat the negative impact of workplace bullying?"

I had to grow up and become a mature Christian. I read cases in the Bible of believers who failed and succeeded. I also identified the origin of the attacks. The individuals did not act alone. A negative spirit influenced them to lash out. So, I researched the history of Lucifer, also known as Satan. It was crucial to learn his characteristics and the personality types he used to attack believers in the past. We must know who we are fighting against. God will position us to defeat Satan.

Conversely, I examined myself. I assessed my strengths and weaknesses. Keeping track of my progress was life changing. Knowing my strengths enable me to be more effective when dealing with adversity on my job. God directed me to fight Satan on the battlefield where I have an unfair advantage, in prayer. Prayer is the only place Satan is prohibited. His VIP (very important perpetrator) pass does not work in your prayer closet. We connect to God quickly and securely without interference. Later in the book, I discuss the different types of prayers and when to use them.

My transformation enabled me to be a change agent against workplace bullying. I soon discovered I was not the only target. Other coworkers, who did not identify as Christians, were also attacked. God used me to speak out against the perpetrators when others were intimidated, which brought positive changes to the workplace. However, I learned Satan never takes a day off. He looks for other areas in our lives where he can attack. Although I overcame workplace bullying, he attacked my family. I applied the same strategies used to overcome bullying on my job. It proved effective to counter any form of adversity.

Secondly, Satan never changes up his schemes. The seasons of attack may change, but the tactics remain the same. In other words, he is predictable. If we stay calm and observe him when he assaults us, then we can recognize his patterns. We must carefully observe the type of individuals used by Satan and the conditions. It is cyclical and you can pretty much predict when he will strike. He works in seasons, places and through people. When we resist him, he must retreat, but it's a guarantee he will return.

This book shares my experiences in dealing with the ultimate bully, Satan, who will attack you anywhere. However, Christ used my negative experience as an opportunity to minister to the victims and perpetrators of the bullying. As Christians, we do not have to be counted among the hundreds of people who lost their jobs, health and peace. We are a chosen generation and must represent Christ as his righteousness in a contentious environment.

I wanted to quit my job. On any given day, I was ready to write my resignation letter. One day the Holy Spirit said, "No you can't quit. This is your proving ground. You must defeat your lion and bear just like King David." His words changed my perspective. I knew I had to overcome my fears to help others. It was no longer about me, but about the Kingdom of God.

David learned to protect his father's sheep in the pasture away from everyone else. God isolated him for greatness. His ability to defend the sheep gave the skills needed to speak out against the enemy of Israel, his nation, and God's people.

Likewise, we endure personal hardships to become a change agent for God. He will use our testimonies to empower others. Romans 8:28 states, "And we know that all things work together for good to them that love God, to them who are the called according to his purpose." (KJV).

Introduction

Everyone handles challenges in their lives differently. Some believe in retail therapy, while others indulge in their favorite comfort food. Avoiding confrontation was my coping mechanism for the challenges I encountered on my job. As an urban planner, I worked in private firms and public agencies for over twenty years. My job entailed dealing with professionals, lawmakers and citizens. Over the course of my career I experienced some highlights, such as successfully completing controversial projects. I also had some low points, which included dealing with workplace bullying.

Workplace bullying, as defined by the **Workplace Bullying Institute (WBI),** is "the repeated, health-harming mistreatment of one or more persons (the targets) by one or more perpetrators." It is abusive conduct, which is threatening, humiliating and intimidating, and includes work interference – sabotage – preventing work from being done or verbal abuse.

The 2014 U.S. Workplace Bullying Survey conducted by the Workplace Bullying Institute reported that more than 36 million American workers directly experienced workplace bullying. Specifically, 60% of the targets for workplace bullying were women.

I tried to deal with the bullying by avoiding the individuals who targeted me. If I had issues with a co-worker, then I retreated within my office. However, when a person of authority interfered with my ability to do my job, I could no longer hide. What began as a few misplaced reports snowballed into work sabotage and missed assignments. I was forced to deal with the bullying directly.

The breaking point for me was the day I was copied on an email. One of my supervisors emailed a staff member at an outside agency. In short, the supervisor blamed me for missing a deadline for a report that was never given to me as an assignment.

I refused to accept the label of incompetence that was placed upon me. Although I was concerned about losing my job, I had to take action by speaking out, and it was necessary to expose the bullying to the entire staff. As I sought God in prayer, he reassured me that I was doing what was right. I was led to talk with other staff members and learned they were having similar problems.

During the staff meeting the following day, I waited patiently for the top supervisor to address the issue. He glossed over it with the "we'll do better next time" speech. Once he finished, I raised my hand to make a statement. I said, "Blaming staff for the mistakes made by management to an outside agency is not acceptable. We are professionals and know how to do our jobs without being undermined."

As I spoke, it was if I grew ten-feet-tall. All eyes were on me, and I felt the presence of God saturate the conference room. I remained composed, and as I ended I looked around the room at the faces of other staff members. There was a silent pause, and then suddenly each one spoke out about their concerns.

God used me to open up the discussion and expose the problem of intimidation raging through our office. Since staff was unified, the supervisors not only apologized, but made some adjustments in the way they treated the staff.

Prior to my successful stand against bullying, I allowed the actions of the bullies to impact my life in a negative way. I did not know how to constructively deal with the pressure. At one point, I'd reached a point in my career that I wanted to just quit my job. However, God showed me how to help my bullies while getting for myself peace of mind in the midst of the turmoil. I learned that the **purpose** of my life was greater than my current problem.

As a result, I embarked on a transformational journey to become a winner in the workplace, rather than a victim. My personal relationship with God was the foundation to create a system of tools and techniques I used to overcome workplace bullying and other life challenges.

In the following chapters, I share these techniques to empower others to effect change in their lives and working environments. As Christian women in the workplace, we should be able to positively change a negative environment without using under-handed tactics.

Understanding my strengths was important because a part of workplace bullying involves the bully trying to make us doubt our abilities. A personal SWOT (Strengths, Weaknesses, Opportunities and Threats) analysis was pivotal to my success because it forced me to look at the areas in my life that needed to change. Methods such as the ten-minute prayer, five-minute confession and maintaining good documentation were strategies I used to help me defeat the bullying on my job.

As I continued my personal development, I realized that my true adversaries weren't the bullies. Many of them needed help in areas of their own lives. As a believer in God, my natural adversary was Satan. The bibles states in James 4:7: "Submit yourselves therefore to God. Resist the devil, and he will flee from you" (KJV). It is important to recognize the tactics of the adversary and counteract them by using prayer and the Word of God effectively.

In the chapters that follow, I provide the profile of Satan from a biblical perspective. You will understand his patterns and learn to recognize his schemes. I Corinthians 10:3-4 states: "For though we walk in the flesh, we do not war according to the flesh. For the weapons of our warfare are not carnal but mighty in God for pulling down strongholds" (NKJV).

Understanding the spiritual source of bullying enabled me to fight against it with prayer, as opposed to shouting it out with a coworker or boss as I had done in the past. I obtained inner joy and peace. As I demonstrated above, God gave me the authority to help others by igniting change in a negative work environment.

Chapter One

KNOW THYSELF

A first-line of defense against the attack of Satan is to know who we are. Understanding our strengths, weaknesses, opportunities and threats (a personal SWOT analysis) is a good start. As working women, for any situation or project the first step is to analyze. Likewise, we must use a similar approach for our personal development as Christians. The SWOT analysis considers the internal and external forces that impact us.

Internal components, for example, include our skills, values and characteristics unique to us. It's what we observe about ourselves and consists of strengths and weaknesses. External components include opportunities and threats. Forces that are outside of our control can either benefit us or block our progress.

The definitions are as follows:

- Strengths – Advantages and unique characteristic. Things we do best.
- Weaknesses – Characteristics or habits that hind you from being your best self.
- Opportunities – Areas where you can utilize your strengths.
- Threats – Areas that will hurt your ability to move forward.

Conducting a personal inventory is a crucial strategy, which shows us areas that need improvement and those we have mastered. If we have a solid understanding of how we think and respond, then we can develop a plan to counteract any attack Satan may launch against us.

Satan doesn't know who we are. He only knows how we respond to confrontations and assaults he has unleashed. However, he seeks to gain intelligence about us to use against us. I Peter 5:8-9 states: "Be alert and of sober mind. Your enemy the devil prowls around like a roaring lion looking for someone to devour. Resist him, standing firm in the faith, because you know that the family of believers throughout the world is undergoing the same kind of sufferings" (NIV). Satan's goal is to formulate a strategy of attack— a kind of playbook of tactics to try and destroy us, our families and our careers.

Seeking to gain the characteristics of the spirit, such as meekness, gentleness, is our best counter against him. It must be a priority. The bible states: "For we are the circumcision, who worship God in the spirit and rejoice in Christ Jesus, and have no confidence in the flesh" (Philippians 3:3 KJV). In this Scripture, it explains that as believers we must serve God in the Spirit without depending only on our natural abilities. We fight effectively in the Spirit because Satan was defeated when Christ died, rose and ascended to heaven. The honing the fruit of the Holy Spirit is our unfair advantage.

Creating a map of all of our characteristics, including strengths and weaknesses, is a starting point for transformation. In the book, "Now, Discover Your Strengths," the author states: "If you want to change your life so that others may benefit from your strengths, then change your values."[1]

For example, as a new staff member in a planning agency I had to work with one of the senior planners to complete an analysis of a neighborhood that was slated for a controversial development project. My strength of collaboration was a direct conflict with the senior planner, who normally worked on projects alone.

We clashed immediately as I attempted to work with him and follow his lead, while he resisted and sought to do things on his own. The conflict went on for weeks, and instead of making my

---

[1] *Now Discover Your Strengths*, Marcus Buckingham and Donald O. Clifton, Ph.D., 2001. Simon and Schuster Inc. p 44.

supervisors aware of my challenges, I tried to work through it and gain some common ground.

On the other hand, the senior planner made a formal complaint about me to our supervisors. As a result, I appeared to be the difficult co-worker. A few months later, my patience wore thin when he accused me of modifying his report without permission. For the record, I did not change anything. Upset, I erupted in a verbal confrontation with him stating, "I don't have to take this anymore; I am seven months pregnant." Needless to say, I did not receive any support from my supervisors, but was required to attend a full-day anger-management course.

The take away from my story is to never allow anyone to determine who we are as an individual. Being slapped with the label of *angry* challenged me to shore up my strengths. I examined myself. I decided to change my life instead of blaming others.

Everything we do must emanate from the Spirit of God, with sincerity. As Christians, we serve as examples to others. In the next section I will share my process for a personal SWOT analysis. Changing our values to those of God, through Christ Jesus will enable us to work within our strengths under the guidance of the Holy Spirit.

Section 1: Personal Inventory

As you begin your personal assessment, take the time to observe how you respond to situations throughout the day. At the end of the day record in a journal how you reacted to something that was enjoyable or stressful. Being mindful of your reactions to situations identifies the areas of improvement.

Reflect on a situation where you had a positive outcome. Write down the strengths used, if any to reach the positive outcomes. Do the same for an unfavorable outcome. Think of what you could have changed to improve the situation, if anything.

If you exhausted all options, but the outcome was still not favorable, write it down. Congratulate yourself for being persistent. As you move forward, don't judge yourself, but take a mental note of your responses and approaches to situations. Compare it against the characteristics of the Spirit. We must take small steps to improve.

We want to make positive changes in our lives to continue our spiritual growth. The next step is to be introspective. We must force ourselves to look past the façade many of us wear to hide our deficiencies as well as true strengths.

Strengths	**Empathy**
Weaknesses	**Argumentative**
Opportunities	**Help former bullies with their personal problems**
Threats	**Bullying**

Working over a thirty-day period, we can identify our strengths, weaknesses, opportunities and threats. Personal development is a process, so making changes will take some time. Studies have shown that changing habits can take anywhere from 18 to 254 days[2]. I will provide you with a guideline I used to change my values and overcome my weaknesses as well as operate within my strengths. In addition, I'll share my methods to detox my spirit and re-train my mind to follow the voice of God.

Strengths

In a SWOT analysis for a business, we always identify the characteristics that give the company an unfair advantage over the competition. Likewise, we must take the time to list characteristics that enable us to withstand an attack from our enemy, Satan.

For instance, use a sheet of paper or a journal and create a two-column table. Label the first column *My Strengths*, and the second label *Godly Strengths*. In my analysis, I used the New King James Versions of Galatians 5:22-23 and Colossians 3:12-14 as a reference to list the Godly Strengths I needed. God will empower us as we pay homage to Him by exhibiting the Godly Strengths in our daily lives. Adding God's values to our strengths will help us become invincible.

---

[2] *European Journal of Social Psychology*, "How Are Habits Formed: Modeling Habit Formation in the Real World," Vol. 40, Issue 6, pg. 998-1009, October 2010, Phillippa Lally, Cornelia H.M. van Jaarsveld, Henry W.W. Potts and Jane Wardle.

My Strengths	Godly Strengths
Sincere	Love
Collaborative	Longsuffering
Discrete	Patient
Trustworthy	Peace
Analytical	Gentleness
Honest	Self-Control
	Merciful

For instance, I needed to balance my strength of collaboration with longsuffering and self-restraint. Although I continued to work with my co-worker, being longsuffering would have aided me in withstanding the adversity indefinitely. Dealing with a difficult person means I understood that he/she would not change. I could accept his personality and not allow it to unsettle me.

I placed the list of desired strengths on my desk where only I could see it. It was a constant reminder of the values I was working to obtain. Every two weeks I was able to check off the values I was able to incorporate into my life. For instance, peace was one of the major values for me to get. I learned how to quiet my mind to focus on things at hand. I will share my method for obtaining peace below.

Fasting

A word of caution, please be prayerful and check with a physician prior to starting a fast. The existence of medical conditions and/or a medical history may impact our ability to go without food and water. I am sharing my personal approach to fasting as an example and not giving any advice.

Fasting was essential to transform my way of thinking. In addition, I altered my daily routine to obtain the new strengths I desired. I selected times in the day to fast[3] and pray. Individuals of various religious backgrounds use the techniques of fasting and prayer to discipline their bodies to bring their minds into subjection.

Traditionally, the Jewish people would pray and fast publicly with dramatic displays of grief when faced with adversity. In some cases, they tore their cloths, cried loudly, put on sack cloth[4] and poured ashes on their heads to express remorse and grief (Ester 4:3 KJV).

---

[3] *Vine, W. Dictionaries*: Fast, Fasting. Blue Letter Bible. Last Modified 24 Jun, 1996.
http://www.blueletterbible.org/search/Dictionary/viewTopic.cfm defines the verb as: to abstain as a religious exercise from food and drink: either entirely, if the fast lasted but a single day, or from customary and choice nourishment, if it continued several days.

[4] Manser, Martin H., *Dictionary of Bible Themes*, BibleGateway.com, 2009, 6742 Sackcloth is a coarse, black cloth made from goat's hair that was worn together with the burnt ashes of wood as a sign of mourning for personal and national disaster, as a sign of repentance and at times of prayer for deliverance.

On the other hand, Jesus Christ taught his disciples to pray and fast discretely instead of publicly showing God their penitence. He advised them to put a small amount of oil on their foreheads and then wash their faces. He states in Matthew 6:18: "...so that you do not appear to men to be fasting, but to your Father who is in the secret place; and your Father who sees in secret will reward you openly" (NKJV).

I deviated from the traditional fast of 16-24 hours and fasted for only 10 hours a day. I fasted daily for at least 30 days. Results may vary, so timeframe maybe adjusted as needed. The biblical meaning of the number 10 is perfect and divine order[5]. Essentially, I was led to fast according to the way God desired instead of setting my own timeframe.

Additionally, I had a history of hypoglycemia (low blood sugar) and going without food and water for extensive amounts of time was hazardous to my health. So, as I sought guidance from the Holy Spirit, He led me to fast from 12 midnight until 10 am the next day.

Skipping my morning coffee and breakfast sandwich was tough at first. However, I was able to clear my mind and turn inward to hear my thoughts. It also allowed me to hone in on hearing from God without being distracted.

Initially, it was difficult to forsake the traditions passed down by beloved pastors and spiritual mentors. However, I learned that in

---

[5] Michael E. Hunt, "The Significance of Numbers in Scripture." AgapeBibleStudy.com, 1998, Revised 2007.

order to be successful in my transformation, it was not about pleasing man or following religious traditions. It was more important to be obedient to the voice of God through the leading of the Holy Spirit.

Also, controlling my reactions was easier. Fasting increased my capacity to be patient with others. The discipline of fasting enabled me to rely on the Holy Spirit instead in my natural reactions.

Prayer

The next tool I utilized was prayer. It is the most effective medium to communicate with God. According to a 2013 study by the Pew Research Center, 55% of American adults make prayer a part of their daily routines. In addition to fasting, prayer was a major part of my morning routine. As a busy mom, carving out an hour for me seemed overwhelming. Initially, I started with 10 to 15 minutes a day and increased it over time. I wanted to form the habit and use smaller increments I knew I could maintain.

Prayer is a time to personally connect with God outside of our hectic schedules. God wants to interface with us. In the book, *A Call to the Secret Place,* Michal Ann and James W. Goll states: "The fact is that God calls every one of us to prayer. The thing we must realize, however, is this: Before God calls us to prayer, He calls us to Himself." [6]

---

[6] *A Call to the Secret Place*, Michal Ann and James Goll, 2003. Treasure House. p 20.

As I spent more personal time with God, it was easier to find windows of opportunity to pray. I unloaded all of the negative energy that built up within me from past events. As I released that energy, I was able to draw from the rejuvenating flow of energy of God.

In Chapter 5, I provide a detailed outline of the prayer I utilized to effectively communicate with God. I also used this time to thank God for all the things He had already done in my life, i.e. family, job, friends, etc. I avoided complaining about co-workers or making personal requests.

Although I was in need of some items, my focus was to receive the intangible things of God instead of material possessions. I opened myself to receive His love. The short steps included the following:

1. One Minute Confession – Tell Christ about a situation that was hurtful.
2. Give Thanks – Express your gratitude to Christ for your life and the little things.
3. Praise – Verbally express my joy for having Christ in my life.
4. Worship – Reverence Christ for being my savior, regardless of what he has done for me.

A positive attitude coupled with gratitude positions our prayers to be answered by God. He is drawn to people who appreciate Him. But complainers alienate themselves from the benefits of peace and joy God desires to bestow upon them.

Study Time

I began my prayer by reading a passage of scripture to nourish my spirit. It also allows for a smooth transition for prayer to guidance. A tablet or smartphone with a bible mobile application kept close by will enhance the prayer experience. "And of course, it is also important that we mediate on God's Word because through His Word, God builds up our faith by revealing Himself to us."[7] The more we learn of God, the easier it becomes to follow Him.

Reading the written Word of God also builds the base of knowledge used in decision making instead of our own intellect. It is important to know the Word of God for ourselves without the filter of others. The bible states in Psalms 119:105: "Your word is a lamp to my feet and a light to my path" (KJV).
Godly wisdom is obtained by studying the bible as well as being directed by the Holy Spirit. In my experience, God confirmed what he instructed me to do during prayer with his written word.

Keeping notes is beneficial to our personal development. We are able to see the progress made towards our goals. It gives us a written record of the direction God wants us to take in our lives. I documented the scriptures in my journal so I could reference them later.

---

[7] *A Call to the Secret Place*, Michal Ann and James W. Goll, 2003, Treasure House, p 21.

Lastly, I wrote my favorite scriptures that helped me boost my confidence on sticky notes and placed them at my desk in my home and on the job. I kept His word before me as a boost to my spirit. It also helped me to stay focused on the strengths I needed to obtain.

At the end of two weeks I reviewed the list and marked off the traits I had mastered. The discipline of prayer and fasting enabled me to become more patient and gain the peace of mind I needed.

We must use the Word of God as our measuring stick and standard of living. Studying the Word of God provides a solid foundation to rebuild our personalities and gain new strengths. In the world system, some traits are viewed as positive, but it's not necessarily so for Christians. Manipulation, intimidation and undermining our peers or co-workers may help us get back at the bullies we face, but such behaviors displease God.

As we grow closer to God, it becomes difficult to act out like others. We are bonded to him through his love for us. My relationship with God helped me to think before reacting to situations. We are the children of God and represent him. We cannot operate as non-believers, but must exude the characteristics of Christ.

Challenges, such as bullies, become easier since we have studied the Word of God and understand how to handle situations accordingly. For instance, if a co-worker raises his/her voice and begins to argue, we must stay calm and lower our voices when responding. The bible states in Proverbs 15:1: "A soft answer turneth away wrath: but grievous words stir up anger."

Furthermore, the teachings of Jesus Christ are sometimes overlooked by many in the religious world. However, in the book of Matthew Chapter 5 he provides the godly characteristics that individuals should possess to represent righteousness.

> Blessed are the peacemakers: for they shall be called the children of God.
> Blessed are they which are persecuted for righteousness' sake: for theirs is the kingdom of heaven.
> Blessed are ye, when men shall revile you, and persecute you, and shall say all manner of evil against you falsely, for my sake (Mathew 5:9-11).

We have the Holy Spirit residing in us. We are temples of God, so we can master our natural minds and DNA to be Christ-like (2 Corinthians 5:17 KJV).

Journaling

Document your experiences in a notebook or nice bound journals—paperback or hard cover and create a "Prayer Journal." In the journal, always write the date, the scripture that you were led to read and the takeaways from your prayers. Most times, if I had an idea or was given specific instructions for an issue I recorded it so I would not forget. You may also record your SWOT analysis with a page dedicated to the specific areas you need to improve. This will serve as a tool to help you identify your character traits. We will also use this journal to help others, which I will talk about in the next section.

Exercise #1: Godly Behaviors - Know Our Strengths

We must take time to master Godly values as describe as the fruits of the spirit as stated above. Our strengths combined with Godly values protect from image Satan attempts to project upon us. The formula for our success is, **our strengths + Fruits of the Spirit = Godly Behaviors.** In a prayer journal list, at least ten things you consider strengths according to Galatians 5:22-23. "But the fruit of the Spirit is love, joy, peace, longsuffering, gentleness, goodness, faith, meekness, temperance: against such there is no law."

When Satan projects thoughts of doubt or degradation into our minds, we'll use what we've written to reject the hurtful thoughts. Based on our list, we'll know what he is saying is a bold-face lie, and it is not a part of who we are in Christ.

Another technique is to use self-encouragement by speaking words to uplift ourselves. "The tongue has the power of life and death, and those who love it will eat its fruit" (Proverbs 18:21 NIV). Life and death in this context refers to speaking from an optimistic perspective or a pessimistic perspective.

Self-encouragement can be described as a type of autosuggestion, which is the medium that utilizes the human senses to impact the subconscious mind. Napoleon Hill, author of *Think and Grow Rich*, states on page 59: "Autosuggestion is the agency of control through which an individual may voluntarily feed his subconscious mind on thoughts of a creative nature, or by neglect, permit thoughts of a destructive nature to find their way into this rich garden of the mind." As we speak our thoughts aloud, they penetrate our minds and subsequently influence the actions we take.

Individuals who have overcome adversity believe in themselves and know that regardless of their current situation, they'll persevere. In the book, *Good to Great: Why Some Companies Make the Leap*, Jim Collins talks about the Stockdale Paradox named after Admiral Jim Stockdale, who was imprisoned eight years in the "Hanoi Hilton," a prisoner-of-war camp during the Vietnam War. He was the highest-ranking U.S. military officer in the camp. The Stockdale Paradox is defined as: "Retain faith that you will prevail in the end, regardless of the difficulties. And at the same time, confront the most brutal facts of your current reality, whatever they might be."

Admiral Stockdale endured brutal conditions, continuous torture and beatings. Despite his current conditions he had unwavering faith that he would not only make it out of the camp, but his ordeal would become a life-defining moment. He states: "This is a very important lesson. You must never confuse faith that you will prevail in the end—which you can never afford to lose—with the discipline to confront the most brutal facts of your current reality whatever they might be." [8]

Admiral Stockdale put his faith into action by creating a non-verbal communication system that enabled him to talk to other prisoners with a series of tapping on the prison walls as a strategy to counteract the isolation and despair. We can embrace this same philosophy knowing that God has equipped us with the tools to overcome any tactic or abuse that the adversary brings our way. Yes, we are currently being targeted by the boss or co-workers, but we must know that regardless of the way we're treated we'll achieve our goals in the end.

One of my favorite scriptures deals with self-perception. Proverbs 23:7a states: "For as he thinketh in his heart, so is he." So, our words can determine the outcome of our situations based on how we perceive ourselves.

In the face of rejection, a non-Jewish woman from Canaan believed that Jesus Christ could heal her daughter. Initially he resisted her request because she was not Jewish. Regardless of what Jesus said, she maintained her confidence. Jesus responded to her in Matthew 15:26-28: "But he answered and said, 'It is not meet to take the children's bread, and to cast it to dogs.' And she said, 'Truth, Lord: yet the dogs eat of the crumbs which fall from their masters' table.' Then Jesus answered and said unto her, 'O

---

[8] *Good to Great: Why Some Companies Make the Leap and Others Don't*, Collins, Jim. Page 85.

woman, great is thy faith: be it unto thee even as thou wilt.' And her daughter was made whole from that very hour."

Our confidence will determine how God responds to us. The woman's persistence captured the attention of Jesus, but her confidence positioned her to receive the blessing. God is looking for believers who will be resilient in the face of adversity. Placing our trust in Him regardless of the conditions will make us victorious.

I've noticed that pessimistic individuals love to be around others similar to themselves. Some of us have walked into the conference room or stumbled upon a small group of women huddled in a corner sneering at folks in the room. They love the fruit of their negative conversations. It reminds me of the mean girls standing in the hallway between classes sneering at anyone that wouldn't become their mindless sidekicks. Likewise, in the workplace, bullies often dominate targets and threaten to alienate them from their group.

However, as Christians—who choose to speak life—we have the authority to speak to our situations and have a positive impact. We can pray for those individuals and ask the Lord to heal their hearts. Perhaps they are dealing with insurmountable situations at home or in their personal lives, and bullying others is an outlet for them. When I discern an unfriendly environment, I pray within myself, "Father, make my adversary my advocate," and the atmosphere is changed from hostile to inviting.

Affirmations or positive self-talk may seem like silly things to do. However, training ourselves to have a positive outlook in the face of adversity will eventually give us the confidence to change a situation simply by speaking to it with faith in God's ability to change the outcome.

In Mark 11:23 Jesus told his disciples: "For verily I say unto you, that whosoever shall say unto this mountain, be thou removed, and be thou cast into the sea; and shall not doubt in his heart, but shall believe that those things which he saith shall come to pass; he shall have whatsoever he saith." Faith in action is power that as believers in Jesus Christ we possess. If we speak in the affirmative and believe it, we can impact the situation.

Exercise #2: Know Our Weaknesses

Similarly, we must write down in our prayer journals our perceived weaknesses and areas we need to improve. Hebrews 6:1a teaches: "Therefore let us move beyond the elementary teachings about Christ and be taken forward to maturity..." (NIV). We should always deal with our downside as well as the upside so we can achieve balance in our development as Christians.

I simply took some sticky notes and wrote the characteristics that I needed to get rid of, such as having a forward mouth (smart mouth) and being argumentative or defensive. Again, I posted it in my work area as a reminder of my goal to improve in those areas. I also kept track of the weaknesses in a prayer journal so I could check off the traits I was able to overcome.

This exercise is designed to strengthen us and to provide a realistic picture of where we are in Christ. Please don't feel condemned or discouraged. The Bible states in James 1:25: "But whoever looks intently into the perfect law that gives freedom, and continues in it—not forgetting what they have heard, but doing it—they will be blessed in what they do" (NIV).

This self-examination is intended to help us look into the Word of God to rebuild our hearts, minds and souls. As Christian women in the workplace, we are challenged constantly. It is hard enough to deal with the pressures in a male-dominated environment in addition to dealing with other women, who mimic the same bullying behavior.

According to the 2014 U.S. Workplace Bullying Survey conducted by the Workplace Bullying Institute[9], 57% of bullies were men and 31% of bullies were women. However, 68% of women targets were bullied by other women, as opposed to only being 57% of targets bullied by men. Thus, women are more than likely to be bullied by other women than men.

Our life in Christ empowers us to be winners if we are aligned with the Word of God that sets us free from the constraints placed upon us in the world. In my case, being argumentative was a weakness I had to overcome. I could not simply fast and pray it away. God took me through a period of time during which He

---

[9] "2014 U.S. Workplace Bullying Survey", Gary Namie, PHD, Research Director, Daniel Christensen and David Phillips, Assistants

commanded me to be quiet. I had to shut-up my big mouth and let the opinions of people that I disagreed with take center stage. It was hard at first, but what I learned was to observe people and their actions.

Satan uses weak individuals to fight against us. Whatever their motivation, we will learn the ways of our attackers by observation. Thus, we will beat Satan at his own game. If we are always defending the bible or our personal beliefs, we cannot observe the approach of your attacker. However, if you take yourself out of the equation and watch how they attack someone else, you will know what their triggers are and how they set up their victims.

Long story short: my season of quietness strengthened me. As a result, I am not easily provoked or moved by aggressive people. I learned how to discern the intent of people. It helped me to determine if I was being baited for an unfruitful argument. I don't know about you, but after being in an argument, I am upset, drained and unproductive. **If Satan could keep me upset all the time and on the defense, then I was not in a position to hear from God.**

Identifying your weaknesses enables you to see how Satan is successful in his attacks. Consequently, we can turn the tables on his strategy by limiting the number of opportunities that Satan can use to take our focus off God. Yes, self-evaluation is painful, but if you go through the exercise and do the work, you will be strengthened to overcome Satan.

Section 2: Breaking Up the Fallow Ground

"Sow to yourselves in righteousness, reap in mercy; break up your fallow ground: for it is time to seek the Lord, till he come and rain righteousness upon you" (Hosea 10:12). This scripture is necessary to understanding how to be a winner in Christ.

Fallow ground is defined as agricultural land left dormant and untilled in order for it to regain its viability. As a result, the land becomes overgrown with weeds, and it's sometimes hard.

As Christians, the composition of our spirits has been transformed by the regeneration of the Holy Spirit. We are comprised of spirit, soul and body (I Thessalonians 5:23). Separating our intellect and natural way of thinking from our regenerated spirit powered by the Holy Ghost is a process orchestrated by God. Our natural abilities and intellect housed in our souls are not needed by God to do his divine will in our lives. Rather, His desire is to break down our soul or the façade to purify our spirits.

In the book, *The Release of the Spirit,* Watchman Nee discusses the importance of breaking down our souls or "outward man" so that God can purify our spirits or "inner man." He states in his book on page 77:

> First, the outward man needs to be broken
> in order to release the spirit. Second, when
> the spirit does come forth, it must not be

33

clouded or muddied by the outward man. This problem takes us further than the mere release of the spirit. It also touches upon the human spirit's clearness and purity.

If one is not enlightened as to the self-centered nature of his outward man and does not judge it strictly before God, instinctively his outward man will involuntarily come out mixed together with his spirit. While he is ministering before God, we can tell that some form of self has come out. He may express God, but he also expresses his un-judged self.

Furthermore, Psalms 51:17 states: "The sacrifices of God are a broken spirit: a broken and a contrite heart, O God, thou wilt not despise." Similarly, we are transformed by the power of the Holy Ghost and our harsh circumstances so that our regenerated spirits will break forth like the sun through a thick blanket of clouds.

Identification of hardened areas in our spirit is vital to destroying the devices of Satan. As experienced Christians, we endure a lot of pain, disappointment and mistreatment from others. It can come from a fellow Christian, a family member, friend or complete stranger. Regardless of the source, we cannot allow the tests and trials we've endured to infiltrate our hearts with bitterness and resentment. The bible guarantees our success against the strategies of Satan.

Isaiah 54:17 states: "No weapon forged against you will prevail, and you will refute every tongue that accuses you. This is the heritage of the servants of the Lord, and this is their vindication from me, declares the Lord" (NIV).

However, we must do the groundwork to keep our hearts clean and our minds clear so we can be winners in Christ. Deuteronomy 10:16 states: "Circumcise therefore the foreskin of your heart, and be no more stiff necked." (KJV) Allowing circumstances to harden our hearts and taint our spirits will result in us resisting God and forming our own opinions and actions. We become inflexible to the call of the Holy Spirit because we have a hardened heart.

I recall when, for a period of time, I separated myself from individuals who were persecuting me. However, I was led by the Spirit to reunite with them. Initially, I resisted because of the previous experience. Once I obeyed all of the hurt, anger and pain that I had experienced at their hands flooded my mind like a tidal wave. It positioned me to confront the real condition of my heart. I had allowed bitterness to overtake me. We can endure so much persecution that it can numb us in areas of our heart.

Once, I realized that I had held in this hurt, I confessed the way I felt at the time of the original occurrence. Instead of staying angry, I made the decision to forgive them. The forgiveness cleansed me and allowed me to heal and move on with my life.

The individuals did not change, but once I confronted the fallow ground in my spirit, I was able to mature and grow as an individual and a believer.

Summary

Self-examination is one of the building blocks to help us mature in Christ. We must not deceive ourselves by ignoring our shortcomings. Our weaknesses are an opportunity for God to strengthen us for his exclusive purpose. Remember to balance your gifts, with the godly characteristics of the Holy Spirit. Our behavior changes when we align our minds and spirit to the written word of God. The power of forgiveness keeps us in the presence of God. We can receive his mercy when we show mercy to others. Below answer the following questions to start your transformation:

1. What are your top 5 strengths?
2. Write down 6 of your weaknesses or areas for improvement?
3. Look at the fruits of the Spirit stated in Galatians 5:22. Write down the virtues you have.
4. Make a list of the virtues in Galatians 5:22 you need.
5. In a journal or notebook write down at 4 things you did right each day. Keep a track of your progress.

Chapter Two

STAY AT THE TOP OF YOUR GAME

In our careers or professions, many of us already have a regimen that helps us stay on top of our game. The same applies to our spirits and relationships with Christ. Part of our daily routine should include self-examination, purification and communication, which I will cover in another chapter. The purification process enables us to drill down to the very essence of our spirits. Thus, we are in a position to receive the instructions and directions we need to be winners. It is hard to hear from Christ when our minds are cluttered with unproductive and negative thoughts.

Purification of our spirits empowers us to move with agility to be effective in anything we do. So, we must lay aside the weights that can overwhelm us and slow us down.

Hebrews 12:1 states: "Wherefore seeing we also are compassed with so great a cloud of witnesses, let us lay aside every weight, and the sin which doth so easily beset us, and let us run with patience the race that is before us." Hebrews Chapter 11 gives an impressive account of the resilient men and women who were successful as believers in God (Hebrews 11:1-39).

As our forerunners in the faith, many did not have the benefits of the guiding indwelling of the Holy Spirit to lead them, but followed the voice of God. They witnessed the manifestation of God in the earth through numerous miracles. Abraham[10], Noah[11], Moses[12], and Rehab[13], faced ridiculous odds, but because of their faith, God worked miracles through them.

We can draw on their experiences to learn how they maintained their faith in spite of the horrendous obstacles. Many were faced with death, but because of their faith achieved unprecedented feats. As New Testament believers, our adversity can be overcome, too. It is inexcusable for us to fail with so many rich examples. God performed awesome works through people that believed in Him.

---

[10] Founding Father of the Nation of Israel. Conceived a son, Isaac, with his wife Sarah who were both over 90 years old. Followed the voice of God to establish a new nation. Genesis 12:1-4 KJV.

[11] Warned by God of the destruction of earth by the flood and built the Arch. Genesis 6:13-27 KJV

[12] Leader God used to bring Nation of Israel out of slavery in Egypt. God performed miracles through him such as the 10 plagues and parting the Red Sea. Exodus 14:13-29

[13] Harlot that hid the spies from Israel in her house. She lived on the great wall of that surrounded the City of Jericho. Joshua 2:22 and Joshua 6:22-25 KJV.

He wants to do the same through us, but we must not allow hindrances to slow us down.

It is hard to run carrying a ton of baggage. The weights in our spiritual lives can include criticism from peers and/or family. Allowing these thoughts to take root and grow within your spirit will taint and eventually alter the way we see ourselves. We must detox our spirits using the Word of God, which brings revitalization.

I will describe for you the common weights of criticism and depression so that you can recognize them when they attempt to overtake your mindset. In addition, I will provide a technique to pull down weights that have become "strongholds" in your mind.

Criticism – Condemning Words from Others

Condemnation is another word for criticism. Often we are so busy seeking the approval of our peers, clients, and family that we internalize their negative remarks. We try to shake them off and keep moving, but deep inside we begin to question ourselves. Soon, we accept the condemning words spoken over our spirits and incorporate those thoughts into our mindsets.

As a result, the negative words have become condemnation, and it attaches itself to our spirits. The reality is that as Christians we are no longer condemned by God, so how can we allow the words of a mere person to condemn us? Romans 8:1 states: "There is therefore now no condemnation to them which are in Christ Jesus, who walk not after the flesh, but after the spirit." We can never allow anyone but the Lord Jesus to define us.

Once we know who we are in Christ, the simple words of negative people can no longer impact our spirits. They are simply words from the bile-filled hearts of people living without the love of God. Their words reflect their spirits and are not a credible critique of us.

Jesus stated in Luke 6:45: "A good man out of the good treasure of his heart bringeth forth that which is good; and an evil man out of the evil treasure of his heart bringeth forth that which is evil: for of the abundance of the heart his mouth speaketh."
In the past, I allowed the negative words of people to impact me because I wanted their approval. Back then, I thought if a negative word was spoken, then it must be true. Well, that was a lie from the pit of hell. Satan uses people to speak hurtful things to you. It is his attempt to project that ungodly image upon your spirit.

Once I had a real understanding of the person that Christ created me to be, those words rolled off me like water hitting a wet suit. As Christians, we are defined by the Word of God, which gives life, power, and peace. II Timothy 1:7 states: "For God hath not given us the spirit of fear; but of power, and of love and of a sound mind." The Word of God stabilizes our spirits and minds so that we are balanced and well-rounded individuals.

Heaviness – A Spirit of Mourning

The last type of weight I will discuss is a mourning spirit. King David exemplifies a man who was not afraid to cry out unto God. He fasted when his infant son, born by Bathsheba[14], was ill. He laid face down seeking God for days. However, once the child died, he got up, ate some food and ended his mourning. In 2 Samuel 5:23 he stated, "But now that he is dead, why should I go on fasting? Can I bring him back again? I will go to him, but he will not return to me."

King David was seeking God for clemency. God through the Prophet Samuel informed him of the child's death (2 Samuel 2:14). Once the child died it was settled. King David accepted it and moved forward with his life. Soon afterwards, he was blessed to have another child with Bathsheba.

Unlike King David, many of us still mourn over dead issues, which God has already forgiven. We refuse to forgive ourselves. Yes, the event was devastating, but at some point, we must allow God to heal us and move forward with our lives. Forgiveness is the first step. This spirit of mourning can become heaviness if we do not seek Christ for deliverance. If we continue to mourn, then we will become stagnate.

---

[14] The soldier Uriah the Hittite's wife, with whom King David committed adultery. Her husband was killed in the war by King David to cover up Bathsheba's pregnancy. 2 Samuel 12:1-14.

The Book of Proverbs states in Chapter 12, verse 25: "Heaviness in the heart of man maketh it stops: but a good word maketh it glad." The Book of Psalms also illustrates the impact of heaviness in Chapter 119, verse 28: "My soul melteth for heaviness: strengthen thou me according unto thy word."

The *International Standard Bible Encyclopedia* defines **heaviness** as what is hard to endure and oppressive. For example, the loss of a loved one or a traumatic event leaves us weighted down. We have to push harder to get things done and are not feeling like our normal selves. I am not dealing with depression, which is defined by the American Psychiatry Association, as a serious medical illness that negatively affects how you feel, the way you think and how you act. According to PsychologyToday.com, "It interferes with daily life, normal functioning, and causes pain for both the person with the disorder and those who care about him or her."

However, for some of us, we are facing situations that we simply cannot handle on our own, and we feel oppressed in our spirits. It is easy for us to minimize feeling blue, down or sad by saying, "I'm in a bad mood today." The spirit of heaviness is not a fruit of the Spirit (Galatians 5:22). Yes, we all have difficult days, but they should not impact the joy that we receive from being loved by Christ. The joy that emanates from the love of God is a perpetual source of strength, which we can draw from when weakened by life's challenges. It is a continuous source of power, but we must learn to pull from it during our darkest days.

Learning to push off the feelings of heaviness from our spirit is fundamental. Our relationship with God is not dictated by our emotions. His joy becomes a part of our core being and saturates our heart. We become resilient through God's love for us. It strengthens us to battle as fearless warriors against any obstacle, even our own emotions. Isaiah 29:19 states: "The humble also shall increase their joy in the LORD, and the poor among men shall rejoice in the Holy One of Israel." [15] Humility is a first step, but God will always boost up our spirits.

When I felt weighted down, I heard the Holy Spirit say, "Push past it." In this case, I utilized the short prayer as outlined in Chapter 1. First step, we must openly confess our feelings to God. It is important to unload the emotions and not internalize them. Being honest about the way we feel allows us to vent and ultimately heal. Second, begin to thank Him for simply being a magnificent God.

As we express our gratitude towards him we step into a realm where joy, peace and love abound. Our emotions can be overpowering, but being appreciative of a Creator who cares about our well-being despite what we feel shows moxie. "Cast your cares on the LORD and he will sustain you; he will never let the righteous be shaken." [16]

---

[15] "Isaiah 29 (King James Version)." Blue Letter Bible. Accessed 7 Jul, 2015. http://www.blueletterbible.org/Bible.cfm?b=Isa&c=29&p=0&rl=0&ss=0&t=KJV
[16] "Psalms 55 (King James Version)." Blue Letter Bible. Accessed 7 Jul, 2015. http://www.blueletterbible.org/Bible.cfm?b=Psa&c=55&p=0&rl=0&ss=0&t=KJV

End the two-minute prayer with a dance, which takes us to another dimension in the process. It is a great ending to a liberating experience. The physical act of dancing is a stress reliever on its own.

God delights in our outward expression of joy. It is fitting to rejoice in the presence of God. Psalms 143:9 states: "Let them praise his name in the dance: let them sing praises unto him with the timbrel and harp." [17] King David danced before the presence of God with such vigor that he danced down to his undergarments (2 Samuel 12-15). [18]

Another remedy for heaviness is found in a scripture verse that is familiar to many of us, the Book of Isaiah 61:3: "To appoint unto them that mourn in Zion, to give unto them beauty for ashes, the oil of joy for mourning, the garment of praise for the spirit of heaviness; that they might be called trees of righteousness, the planting of the Lord, that he might be glorified."

The first time I read this scripture, I was enduring a very dark time in my life. I was getting over the loss of a personal relationship. My spirit was broken and I could not find a reason to be joyful about anything. Once I read the passage, I felt relieved. I was at work in an isolated area of the building. I remember taking off my suit jacket, which represented the sadness I felt, and threw it to the

---

[17] "Psalms 149 (King James Version)." Blue Letter Bible. Accessed 7 Jul, 2015. http://www.blueletterbible.org/Bible.cfm?b=Psa&c=149&p=0&rl=0&ss=0&t=KJV

[18] "2 Samuel 6 (King James Version)." Blue Letter Bible. Accessed 7 Jul, 2015. http://www.blueletterbible.org/Bible.cfm?b=2Sa&c=6&p=0&rl=0&ss=0&t=KJV

ground. I was liberated instantly and began jumping around and dancing. I cried because of immediately felt the comfort of the Holy Spirit.

The backdrop of Isaiah 61 portrays the nation of Israel, which formerly embodied the power of God, as desolate and under the authority of another nation (Isaiah 1:7). Babylon, an enemy nation, subdued Israel because of their blatant disregard of God's covenant by generations of Jewish Kings (2 Chronicles 36:6-8). Israel was under the captivity of Babylon for decades, but God did not intend to leave them enslaved forever.

Jerusalem, the capital city of Israel, was also the official place of worship to God by the Jews. Also, known as Zion, it would come to symbolize the new nation of believers to follow God under the authority of Jesus Christ including Jewish and Non-Jewish (Gentiles) people.

Zion [19] would no longer be the physical location, but the Body of believers who serve God in Spirit instead of through sacrifices and traditions. Jesus explained the paradigm shift to the [20] Samarian women he met at the well in the book of John. He stated, in John 4:23: "But the hour is coming, and now is, when the true

---

[19] "BLB - 2Ki 19: Book of 2 Kings 19 (Blue Letter Bible: KJV - King James Version)." Blue Letter Bible. Accessed 11 Sep, 2015. http://www.blueletterbible.org/kjv/2ki/19/31/s_332031
[20] "BLB - John 4: Gospel of John 4 (Blue Letter Bible: KJV - King James Version)." Blue Letter Bible. Accessed 11 Sep, 2015. http://www.blueletterbible.org/kjv/jhn/4/23/s_1001023

worshipers will worship the Father in spirit and truth; for the Father is seeking such to worship Him" (NKJV).

The two-fold message in this chapter promised relief for the Jews' current situation and served as the prediction of the coming Messiah, Jesus Christ, who reconciled mankind to God (Luke 4:17-21). Words of deliverance were sent through the prophet Isaiah to the remnant of Israel.

Specifically, in Isaiah 61:3, the passage provides relief from former weights for modern day Christians, too. God, through Jesus Christ, provides eternal salvation for the Gentiles, who were alienated from God. Due to the discretions of Adam and Eve, eternal life was snatched for mankind. The promise of living forever is not a story line for great fiction, but a benefit from being in a direct relationship with God. Our spirits will live past the current reality to be with God forever (John 17:2).

The deal is sweetened by the fact that we become friends with God, through Jesus Christ. We can experience a personal relationship with Christ, just as Adam and Eve did with God before they were cast out of Eden (Genesis 3:24). Thus, we have access to everything we need as long as we adhere to his written word (John 15:7).

However, constant interaction is essential. It is easy for you to help out a friend whom you talk to on a regular basis. There is nothing you would withhold from them because of your relationship. Likewise, Christ will fulfill our every need because of our relationship with Him. We can ask him with confidence for what we need when under duress because of our rapport. One of my favorite scriptures, Hebrews 4:16 states: "Let us approach God's throne of grace with confidence, so that we may receive mercy and find grace to help us in our time of need" (NIV).

As well, God seeks to deliver us from the stress of our everyday life. As we meditate on the written Word of God, our minds will be cleared of all confusion. If we look at Isaiah 61:3, the two things that capture our attention are joy and praise. Joy represents the Holy Spirit, which is the vessel God uses to directly communicate with us.

Christ foretold of the Holy Spirit, also known as the Comforter, to his disciples before He was crucified for the sins of the world (John 14:17, 26). Although his time on earth was coming to an end, Jesus assured the disciples they would not be left to fend for themselves. The Holy Spirit would be a teacher to instruct them in the ways of God.

Joy is another benefit from the indwelling of the Holy Spirit within our spirit (Galatians 5:22). Anointing oil was traditionally used in a ceremony to establish priests for their life-long service to God in the tabernacle. Christ establishes His believers with the anointing of the Holy Spirit (John 4:24). The Holy Spirit is the embodiment of God's nurturing spirit and brings us joy to offset the rough circumstances we encounter in life. Joy is defined as a feeling of pleasure or happiness that comes from a sense of well-being.

Also, known as one of the ten positive emotions in some psychology circles, joy energizes us regardless of momentary circumstances. We are assured God is moving behind the scenes to create the best outcome for us. Instead of feeling stuck, we can express our joy through the physical act of praise, including dancing, singing and speaking. The garment of praise is the outward expression of the attributes we obtain from our relationship with God. He is the source of our strength and protection.

The spirit of praise, like a crest on a blazer, can be used to identify believers in Christ. The adorning of a blazer with a crest identifies the individual associated with a culture, organization or country. Likewise, our praise of God identifies us with Christ. Praise is mandated as a strength-building exercise, which fortifies our inner spirit and keeps us continually connected to the presence of God.

 Members of certain organizations wear jackets with a crest representing their values, and they are immediately associated with prestige, honor and exclusive access to events not open to the public. An example for the sports enthusiasts is the coveted green blazers for winners of the Professional Golf Association (PGA) Masters' Tournament, or the yellow blazers for National Football League (NFL) Hall of Fame. They are Very Important People (VIP) and allowed to go beyond the red-velvet ropes.

Our praise gives us access to God's presence, and we should always be adorned with it (Psalm 107:2). As we reside in His presence we can enjoy a supernatural experience and receive the healing, insight or serenity we crave.

Accordingly, the transformation of our inner spirits will manifest in our outward appearance. As we exude peace on the inside, we will portray a confidence that was not there in the past. God will establish us as his examples to others. Isaiah 61:3 describes the rejuvenated people of God as the trees [21] of righteousness. Trees are figurative of vitality and strength. We will stand tall, with our roots deeply planted in the Word of God as we grow as Christians.

Conversely, our godly traits can make us targets of others, who seek to do things in an unjust manner. Personal attacks are a part of having strong ethics in the workplace. Individuals that follow the rules, unwilling to compromise their ethics are called rigid. We are still covered by Christ because He is our mediator with God and man. He directs the Holy Spirit to provide a strategy for us to maneuver around the false accusations of others. Later in the book, I will discuss in detail the traits of our primary enemy Satan, who is the true accuser of the believers in Christ.

The reason we have access to such life-changing resources is simply because God loves us. It was never his intention for mankind to be without direct access to eternal life. Consequentially, Jesus Christ was sent to save the world, not to condemn it (John 3:19). So, we have unmerited favor with God. It

---

[21] Easton, M. "Dictionaries: Teil Tree." Blue Letter Bible. Last Modified 24 Jun, 1996. http://www.blueletterbible.org/search/Dictionary/viewTopic.cfm

is his grace that provides us with a plan for a better life in our current situation and beyond.

Yes, life-changing incidents can occur in our lives. We question if God is still with us. However, being grateful for the things we still have lifts our spirit and helps shift our attention towards something more positive. Continuing to express negative emotions, such as fear and doubt, limits our ability to rebound. Focusing on the downside of the situation takes away our ability to have an open mind to see possible solutions.

A hostile work environment, for example, can be difficult for some to navigate. However, as we continue to express joy despite the conditions, we become like a healthy tree with deep roots, unshaken by the storms dusting up around us. Others will intentionally seek us out because of our resilience.

In closing, I want to pose a question to you. Write down some times in your life when you had to set a godly example and proved to be "a righteous tree of life?" Who do you give the credit for your ability to be resilient? If you received criticism for your actions, who do you think should speak on your behalf?

A Spirit of Thanksgiving

Another defense against heaviness is maintaining a spirit of gratitude. Taking a moment to reflect on the good times we had in our lives will lift our spirits. This small action will shift our focus off the negativity of the current situation so we can take a moment to regain our composure and think clearly. As our emotions change from feeling negative to being optimistic, we broaden our perspective, which moves us towards a possible solution.

Gratitude is defined as acknowledgment of having received something good from another. Again, showing gratitude to God places us into His presence where we have access to benefits such as adoration, harmony and charity. Being ungrateful, alienates us from Him, and positions us to complain and murmur. History has shown God does not like his people to complain. The children of Israel delivered out of Egypt from slavery who complained did not see the land promised to them. Their ungratefulness forfeited their inheritance to next generation (Numbers 14:27-30).

Yes, the obstacles we face can seem unbearable, such as losing your home, the death of a friend, being laid-off from a job after ten years, or a car accident that leaves you disabled. We must have the courage to take a step back, appreciate what we still have and seek to learn from the adversity.

I have experienced events such as bullying, unemployment and the death of loved ones as I am sure you have, too. The key is remembering we are not alone in our struggles. We can overcome our struggles with finesse. Christ is the missing link to disconnect us from our current situation and connect us to our inheritance to the next generation. The spirit of gratitude positions us to receive the energizing force from him to move forward.

We must come before Christ with a spirit of thanksgiving. He is drawn to the edifying words of our mouths such as thankfulness and adoration. Expressing appreciation for what we presently have plants us firmly in God's presence. We should say the following:

Thank you for giving me another opportunity to see the sun; I am grateful for having a family; I lost my job, but I know you will provide for me; thank you for my raise; I am grateful for having a place to live; thank you for my health; I appreciate you for protecting my children; and thank you for giving me a new business idea.

Our spirits are immediately uplifted because we focus on the good things instead of dwelling on what we don't have. Concentrating on a negative event restricts our ability to see beyond the current situation. We cannot open ourselves to see the possibilities despite the limitations.

Gratitude also sets a stage for learning from the adversity, while preparing us to be courageous. It takes fortitude to think of others while we are enduring difficult times. Being appreciative of what we have positions us to be giving towards others.

So, how do we foster such an attitude in the face of adversity? Simple, we take it one moment at a time. Reflecting on the instances when God demonstrated his favor in our lives provides evidence of his ability to do it again in the future.

For example, the automobile accident that was avoided when you intuitively hesitated at the green light; the neighbor who looks out for your home when you are traveling; the promotion you received on your job; having access to a mentor who gives you great advice; the support of family and friends; the approval of a loan to start a business; and the friend who helps with the children when you have to handle matters at work.

Keeping a daily journal of the things we are thankful for also builds our capacity. The gratitude we have can give us strength to say, "Thank You, God," during the toughest moments of our lives. As we focus less on ourselves, we become free to seek out opportunities to help others less fortunate.

Volunteering with organizations in our community is a perfect way to nurture a spirit of thanksgiving. Being a part of a social cause that positively impacts others can invigorate our spirit. Doing small gestures for strangers, such as opening a door, paying for the coffee of the person in line behind you, provides boosts of positive energy that keeps your spirit charged. The Word of God directs us to give thanks in all things. Despite the severity of events in our lives, we are assured it will benefit us in the long run. We can learn and grow from the positive and negative situations in our lives.

Sure, there are times when we are not in the mood to speak wonderful things. However, the serenity of God enables us to stay grounded regardless of the hardship in our path. We must learn to relish our experience as believers in Christ. Let's take comfort in the fact that everything we endure sets a solid foundation to build us up to flourish. Cherishing every quiet moment, we have with him fuels us to continue our journey with him.

My secret weapon against heaviness is *praise*. There were times when I felt the heaviness of walking in the door of my job, but I said to myself, "I will delight in the Lord for he is my Rock and Fortress." I began to cut a step right in the parking area. I did not care if anyone was looking. If you don't want to dance, then jump for joy. It works better than any energy drink, and the presence of God will come to strengthen your spirit.

We must learn to praise Christ regardless of the circumstances. We can praise Him for situations such as being overlooked for successfully completing a project or meeting a new contact for a business idea, coworkers who try to undermine us on a project, unsupportive family members, difficulty raising teenagers, loyal friends who always have our backs, and an opportunity to interview for a new job.

He will honor our praise and fellowship with us on the spot. It is what the old folks call "A right-now praise." Hebrews 13:15 states: "By Him therefore let us offer the sacrifice of praise to God continually, that is, the fruit of *our* lips giving thanks to his name."

Pulling Down Strongholds – Casting Down Weights

Some instances of heaviness and condemnation are more intense than others. I have experienced heaviness that just hovered over my head like an angry bee looking to sting its next victim. In this instance, the heaviness was attempting to be a stronghold in my spirit. Let's look closer at the word *stronghold*. The Hebrew (Lexicon, 2015) and Greek words for stronghold mean (Dictionary, 2015) *fortress*. In military terms, a stronghold refers to a fortified place to take refuge from the enemy. However, in this case, a stronghold of heaviness is place that becomes fortified within our spirit in which we are trapped. As an alternative to safety, we become prisoners to this fortified way of thinking, which impacts our behavior.

Our place of refuge rests in our confidence in God to follow the leading of the Holy Spirit, as opposed to succumbing to the suppressive influence of the stronghold of heaviness. As I illustrated in the previous sections, preventing heaviness gives us an advantage when we face adversity. However, in cases when the stronghold attempts to attack despite our daily regimen of prayer, joy, gratitude and praise, we still have an arsenal to combat it.

We have authority as Christians in the Spirit to pull down strongholds through prayer. Prayer, detailed in Chapter 5, is the ultimate weapon against the tactics of our enemy to overtake us. Our relationship with Christ provides unlimited resources to address any situation we encounter.

In the previous section I discussed proactive strategies to deal with heaviness. However, the reactive tactics are biblically mandated and effective in dealing with a stronghold.

We are taught in 2 Corinthians 10:3-5:

> 3: For though we walk in the flesh, we do not war after the flesh:
>
> 4: (For the weapons of our warfare are not carnal, but mighty through God to the pulling down of strong holds ;)
>
> 5: Casting down imaginations, and every high thing that exalteth itself against the knowledge of God, and bringing into captivity every thought to the obedience of Christ;

In other words, we can take control of our thoughts and words through prayer. We can speak against the forces trying to overtake our spirits. We cannot use the playground method of yelling expletives or profanity. Instead, we must speak the words given us that are based on the written Word of God and the Holy Spirit.

Case in point: Jesus taught his disciples how to pull down a stronghold. In Matthew 16:19 he states: "And I will give unto thee the keys of the kingdom of heaven: and whatsoever thou shalt bind on earth shall be bound in heaven: and whatsoever thou shalt loose on earth shall be loosed in heaven."

Personally, I've experienced a stronghold of doubt that attempted to overtake me while working in an organization. Of course, when we are new to the workforce, and we've started our first full-time position, we may have some doubts about our job performance.

However, with coaching and working hard we learn the ropes, and that sense of doubt dissipates.

In my case, I was established in my field and had several years of experience. I was challenged constantly by supervisors and senior-level staff on the merits of my work. At times, I would be blamed for misplaced or late reports that I knew I had submitted in a timely manner.

Aside from documenting and backing up all my work files, I took it to God in prayer. First, I identified the type of stronghold I was dealing with, which was doubt. Second, during my morning routine, I confessed my feelings, forgave the individuals involved and showed my gratitude to God for my job.

Third, every day before I arrived at work I'd say the following prayer: "In the name of Jesus, I come against the spirit of doubt, fear and intimidation that is set against me. Lord, make my adversaries my advocates." Lastly, I sealed it with a praise dance by thanking God in advance for the victory over this attempted takeover. I saw the results quickly, as other co-workers voiced similar experiences.

Consequently, the individuals toned down their criticism since the supervisors were made to be accountable for their own actions.

Power of Prayer

As shown above, we can see the power of prayer in action. My request was made know to God, and he responded.

We must be specific in our requests, while being directed by the Holy Spirit for the solution. Prayer is the way we communicate with Jesus Christ through the power of the Holy Ghost (Romans 8:26). There are six types of communication with God that include petitions, supplications, intercessions, penitence (repentance), worship, and thanksgiving (1 Timothy 2:1). Our prayers are a way to fellowship with Christ, such as prayers of worship and thanksgiving. In this case, we verbally express our appreciation for major and minor things he has done in our lives.

Specifically, I want to discuss *supplication* as an effective tool to help us flourish in the workplace. However, the Greek word for supplication is hiketēria, according to Strong's Bible Lexicon and is the feminine noun for the word suppliant—one who humbly approaches a person of a higher authority for favor.

Thus, our prayer of supplication means that we can seek God with an unpretentious spirit and request favor from him to move on our behalf. Being pretentious is a surefire way to get your request ignored. God repels arrogant individuals, but is attentive to those with a humble spirit.

This is a prayer that changed the game for me when I worked in environments where the people in authority showed partiality to individuals based on personality instead of work performance.

Case in point: a former employer held weekly meetings with employees that included a set aside time to freely discuss a variety of topics.

Several employees faithfully served as devil's advocate to shoot down ideas given by others. Most times, the supervisors would give more weight to the opinion of the opposing employees, rather than give it real consideration. In addition, every time I opened my mouth to make a suggestion one particular staff member was always ready with an opposing argument. I felt powerless at times, and rather than being combative, I would remain quiet.

However, I had an idea that just nagged at me, since during that time, the city was getting attention from outside developers for new commercial developments. God gave me an idea for a city-wide project to inventory commercial districts in the municipality. Immediately, I knew the voice of opposition from certain employees would be ready to rebuff me. I did my homework, creating some mock-ups of forms and talked with other individuals in my industry to gather information before bringing it to the table.

The morning of the meeting, I prayed, "Lord give me the boldness to share this idea. Strengthen me to stand up against my adversaries. Prepare me to respond to every question." During the day, I stayed prayerful, while thinking of possible questions I would be asked.

As I pitched my idea that afternoon I could feel the hard stares from the others in the room. As predicted, the one employee pounced on me with a barrage of questions. I made eye contact and responded without blinking. My response quieted the naysayers, and instead of ridicule I received compliments.

Although the project was never implemented, it showed me how prayer and preparation can position me to make an impact in a negative environment. I discovered how an efficacious supplication can pull down the strongholds of doubt, fear and intimidation. As believers, we must fight where we have the advantage, which is in our time of prayer to God. As explained in the classic book, The Art of War, by Sun Tzu, "Attack him where he is unprepared, appear where you are not expected." (Tzu, 2015)

The true enemy is Satan, and he will use the negative attitudes in others to bully us. We should not make it personal as a direct attack from the individual, but recognize the spirit that is in operation around that person.

In the example, above, I did not tell anyone else my idea, so I had an element of surprise. It was hard for someone to effectively attack the idea, since they did not know anything about it. In addition, I maintained an advantaged because of my preparation for the opposition. Lastly, no one expected it from me.

We must position ourselves to be used by God in our places of employment. If you have been pushed into a corner by domineering co-workers, it is time to move to the forefront by allowing God to speak through you. Our ability to pull down strongholds will impact the quality of life for others.

Prayer is also a weapon against the power of Satan. As discussed in the previous section about strongholds, we can make a request to God to protect us from our enemies and also receive results. For example, a former pastor, now deceased, taught me the power of supplication. I would tell him of the mistreatment I was encountering on my job among the support staff (administrative) and supervisors. He said calmly, "We are going to pray that God give you favor within and without the company so that you can be effective on your job."

In other words, we prayed and asked God to give me favor with the executives and the administrative staff since I needed the cooperation of both to do my job. After the Pastor and I prayed together, my reports got done on time, instead of being shoved to the bottom of the stack. I was also given more of a leadership role on projects, where previously I was quietly disregarded.

Jesus told his disciples in Luke 18:7-8a: "And shall not God avenge his own elect, which cry day and night unto him, though he bears long with them? I tell you that he will avenge them speedily." However, we must come with a humble spirit and in peace. Vengeance belongs to God. If we come to God with malice and anger in our hearts against the individuals who have wronged us, we'll be in error (Romans 12:19).

Prayer, however, is useless if we pray outside of the plan of God. He has a plan for his believers, and it is for our total well-being, spiritual, personal and professional. The fastest way to know his plan is to understand his Word. Praying the written Word of God is a tool that Satan cannot counteract. The Sword of the Spirit, which is the written Word of God, discerns the thoughts, heart and intent of man. Ephesians 6 states: "And take the helmet of salvation and the sword of the Spirit, which is the word of God..." (KJV). Understanding the scriptures will unlock a wealth of knowledge and many strategies for success.

Sword of the Spirit -- Word of God

The weapon of the Holy Spirit, who is the Spirit of God, is the very Word of God. Case in point: when Jesus was led by the Spirit into the wilderness to be tempted by the devil he spoke the written Word of God as a defense against Satan's attacks.

The first strike of the devil was to try to appeal to Christ's ego by asking him to prove that he was the Son of God by turning stones into bread. However, Jesus made no reputation of himself, but wanted only to please God the Father. He was not lifted up in pride. He simply replied in Matthew 4:4: ". . . It is written, Man shall not live by bread alone, but by every word that proceedeth out of the mouth of God."

He has shown us that we must live by the spoken Word of God. Notice that the word *proceed* is used because he is speaking about the Word that will continually flow from the mouth of God. Also included is the written Word, which was recorded by holy men who were moved by the Spirit of God, as well as the spoken Word that will come from the Holy Spirit.

The bible tells us in John 16:13: "Howbeit when He, the Spirit of truth, is come, He will guide you into all truth: for He shall not speak of himself; but whatsoever He shall hear, that shall He speak: and He will shew you things to come." This lets us know that whatever proceeds out of the mouth of God, the Holy Spirit will tell us and show us the upcoming events in our lives.

In other words, not only must we study and know the written Word as Jesus himself used it against Satan in the wilderness, but we must also have an ear to hear what the Spirit of the Lord is telling us (Joshua 1:8). Aside from leading us into all truth, the Holy Spirit intercedes for us by helping our infirmities when we pray in the Holy Ghost. Isaiah 30:21 states: "And thine ears shall hear a word behind thee, saying, 'This is the way, walk ye in it, when ye turn to the right hand, and when ye turn to the left.'" The Holy Spirit will guide us around the traps and temptations set up by the devil if we have an ear to hear what the Lord is saying.

One summer, I was home with my youngest daughter who was 18-months-old at the time. My husband took the other kids on a picnic. We went outside and I placed her on the porch so I could get a book from the car, which was parked in the driveway.

I was unaware that my daughter crawled off the porch and was walking behind me. Before I could reach the car, I heard the spirit say, "Turn around and look at Maya." I complied without hesitation and immediately two white pit bull dogs walked from the alley that abutted our home and darted straight for her. I remained calm and walked towards her before they reached her. I slowly picked her up, never showing any fear and quickly walked into the house.

I knew this was divine intervention because the same two dogs had attacked my husband earlier in the week. It was still dark outside as he was leaving for work, but they attacked him unprovoked. He had to run back into the house and wait until they left. Maya and I were basically sitting ducks, since it was the middle of the afternoon on a sunny day. The dogs never barked, even as I retreated to the house. I did not tremble until we were safe inside.

The Sword of the Spirit, or the Word of God, is also described in Hebrews 4:12 as: "For the Word of God is quick and powerful, and sharper than any two-edged sword, piercing even to the dividing asunder of soul and spirit, and of the joints and marrow, and is a discerner of the thoughts and intents of the heart." In other words, the Word of God is living and powerful and will separate our natural thoughts from the spiritual thoughts of the Holy Ghost. The Word of God can discern and decipher the hidden agendas and motives of the heart.

Instant Prayer – Tool to Pull Down Strongholds

Instantaneous prayer is a weapon that many Christians under-utilize. It is optimal for busy women in the marketplace because we do not have time to take a break, find a closet, and send up our prayer to heaven.

The fast pace of the business world mandates quick response, so being instant in prayer is an effective tool to overcome any obstacle Satan throws in our paths. In this case, instant prayer is merely to ask Christ, in His name, to move on our behalf. I must caution you not to ask out of vengeance, but make a clear request in compliance with the Word of God (Romans 12:17-19). Meaning, we are to send positive thoughts to individuals who undermine us. As believers, we have higher standard of integrity.

For example, I was working on a project that was supported by some influential organizations and individuals in the business community. The multimillion-dollar project was going to use the investment dollars of a major municipality's pension fund. Upon my initial review the project seemed routine, but the proposed use was not in line with legal land-use policy.

On the other hand, the residents in the area were highly engaged and aware that the proposed development was not in compliance with the land-use ordinance. After two community meetings, dozens of meetings with the development team and community representatives, I had to stand by my recommendation for denial of the project. I recognized there was a greater force at work and was professional with both the community and the developers. I maintained my integrity by not getting involved personally or showing partiality to anyone.

I will never forget one meeting in which another member of our staff stepped out of the room, and I was left alone with the developer's team of representatives. The demeanor of the lead team member changed from smooth and laid back to serious and domineering. I did not over-react or become emotional, but realized that the spirit of the individual had changed. I was challenged on every point of my recommendation and at one moment personally attacked. I quietly prayed within my spirit, and God helped me stand my ground based on the merits of my research and work.

I swallowed the lump in my throat when the demeanor of the individuals turned from friendly to stern. I felt outnumbered initially, but I was confident in God and myself. I was not a rookie in the field, and I knew a lot was on the line for both sides. Again, I had the element of surprise on my side, because I appeared weak, but had the strength of God within me.

Once the other member of the staff returned, the atmosphere of the room changed again, and the individual returned to being laid-back. I was able to make a joke and say, "Yes, while you were gone they tried to strong-arm me, but it didn't work."

We all laughed, but I knew that the individual was very serious. I was able to identify the shift in the attitude and resist the spirit of intimidation. I ask the Lord, "Strengthen me in this meeting, and I rebuke the spirit of intimidation and doubt." 1 John 5:14-15 states: "And this is the confidence that we have in him that, if we ask any thing according to his will, he heareth us: And if we know that he hear us, whatsoever we ask, we know that we have the petitions that we desired of him."

On the other hand, an instant prayer that would be considered an offensive strategy, in which you are striking out first before Satan can attack, would be as follows:

> "In the name of Jesus, show the hand of the enemy and expose any plot or trap set up against me. I take authority over Satan and his devices right now and put him under my subjection."

This is a prayer that proved effective as I worked on projects with underhanded individuals, who wanted to work outside of the regulations and codes required by the local law.

In the professional world, there are always individuals who want to go around the system. They do not care about your integrity or professionalism, but want to get their projects completed as soon as possible. In addition, I set the parameters of safety around me every day to stop the negative words and actions launched by Satan to throw me off course. This is similar to the firewall that computer programmers use to protect servers and computers against viruses and malware. Such as, "In the name of Jesus Christ, I set a firewall of defense around me to thwart the words of the enemy. Let the negative and ungodly actions of others have no effect on my spirit."

These are short prayers I have used before I enter my place of business, meetings or even family gatherings. Yes, they have proven very effective. I have also prayed these prayers in the midst of meetings and watched the hand of God move on my behalf.

We must recognize the favor and authority that God has given us through Jesus Christ. Being instant in prayer makes you an efficient and high-achieving person. You are able to work with difficult people while maintaining your peace, sanity and integrity.

An example of a defensive instant prayer is one that you must use to change the course of action right at that second. You can pray within your mind a prayer to stop Satan in his tracks. In my profession as an urban planner, I must work with multiple disciplines and professionals to complete projects. I must interact with administrative assistants, lawyers, architects, engineers, and elected officials, etc.

On occasion, I have had to pray that a person being difficult and rude provide me with the information that I needed. I have also had to take authority—while maintaining my composure—when individuals were rude and unprofessional toward me. One of the prayers included the following:

> "I pray in Jesus's name that my adversary become my advocate and provide me with the information that I need right now."

I had to adjust my spirit and look to Christ for help. Sometimes you have to pray for your enemies, as well because people are dealing with their own problems and do not want to be bothered with your requests at that moment.

We must be discerning and understand how to pray so that we can meet our spiritual and professional objectives. Usually I pray, "Lord strengthen their hearts and heal their spirits this very moment. Touch their hearts and give them the peace they need." I have prayed for disgruntled people over the phone without them realizing it, and their moods shifted. Before the end of the phone call, not only did I obtain the information I needed, but they told me to have a nice day.

Summary

Staying on top of our game as we live for Christ is no easy task. We must stay alert to the words of others and our own to avoid the spirits of condemnation and mourning. They become strongholds if we allow them to consume our mind and spirit. Prayer, praise and a spirit of gratitude are tools to refresh our spirits. The attacks from our adversary will never cease, but we can remain vigilante with a consistent prayer life. God gave us the authority over the devices of Satan. All we have to do is put them to use. Instant prayer is the most effective weapon to counteract the negativity felt from individuals who try to intimidate you. Practice the power of praise and gratitude below. Answer the following questions to keep the joy stirred up in your spirit.

1. Name one occasion when God delivered you from dire situation?
2. Explain how it made you feel?
3. Take a praise break and show God your appreciation for what he did for you in the past.

4. Write down a current situation you need God to move on your behalf.

Write a mini-letter and thank him in advance for what he will do in your life.

_____

_____

_____

_____

_____

_____

_____

_____

_____

_____

_____

Chapter Three

KNOW THY ENEMY

Eve, the original working woman, had the first encounter with Satan in the Garden of Eden. I am sure if she had known the characteristics of Satan, she would have made a better choice. Unlike Eve, we have advantages over the tactics of Satan: The Holy Spirit and the written Word of God. Both are tools that empower us to overcome and take the authority over Satan that Christ has given us.

Knowing the characteristics, motivations, and schemes of our enemy delivers a victory into our hands time and time again. You will be able to see the attack before he can even execute it. For instance, in football (bear with me non-sports fans) a good quarterback is able to read the strategy of a defensive team based on the way the players line up at the line of scrimmage. If the quarterback can see that the defensive players are going to rush him, meaning all of the linebackers will run straight at him, then he can make adjustments before the ball is in play.

If we, as Christians, can recognize the shift in our environments, then we will know how to counteract and throw off Satan's scheme. He is very predictable once you understand how he operates. He uses the same strategies constantly. He may change up the times and seasons of attacks, but the scheme will be the same.

In keeping with our football example, it is similar to a football team that runs the same plays for every situation. A football team with a strong running back and quarterback with a weak arm will hand-off the ball instead of throwing a pass. Soon, the defense will know to go after the running back instead of focusing on the wide receivers. As a result, the defensive players are successful at stopping the team from advancing the ball to score a touchdown. Likewise, we can learn the attacks of Satan and understand how to block him from attacking us without being stressed.

Section 1: Background – Lucifer the Fallen Angel

Let's take a step back and learn about the background of Satan. Lucifer, which means Son of Morning, was created by God Almighty as an angel. He was one of the chief Angels over the music in heaven. Seriously, Satan was the Praise Leader in the holy mountain of God, as the bible describes. His body was covered in precious stones, and music emanated from his body.

Ezekiel 28:14-15 states: "You were in Eden, the garden of God; every precious stone *was* your covering: The sardius, topaz, and diamond, Beryl, onyx, and jasper, Sapphire, turquoise, and emerald with gold. The workmanship of your timbrels and pipes was prepared for you on the day you were created. You *were* the anointed cherub who covers; I established you; you were on the holy mountain of God; you walked back and forth in the midst of fiery stones" (NKJV).

Lucifer was a high-ranking angel, who was specially made, a glorious sight to see. He walked among other angels. However, an insatiable appetite for power and ambition became his downfall. He desired to exalt himself over the Almighty God. In essence, he was made a perfect creature until his heart became filled with violence and iniquity.

He was anointed and had great authority, an influential angel in the mountain of God and produced results. Ezekiel 28:16 further states: "By the abundance of your trading you became filled with violence within, and you sinned; Therefore, I cast you as a profane thing; Out of the mountain of God; And I destroyed you, O covering cherub, From the midst of the fiery stones" (NKJV). However, before he was cast out, Lucifer led a rebellion against God in heaven. He wanted to exalt himself to be the ruler over all. He was cast out of heaven along with the angels that followed him. One third of the angels were deceived, and they are currently reserved in chains of darkness. Jesus states in Luke 10:18, "... I beheld Satan as lightning fall from heaven."

Subsequently, Lucifer was transformed to Satan, which means contrary, adversary, enemy and accuser. Satan is our bona fide enemy. In the next section, we discuss three of the major roles he plays as an enemy to God and Christians: accuser (fault finder), deceiver, and tempter (liar).

Section 2: Three Major Roles of Satan

The Bible describes Satan in several different roles, such as a roaring lion, an old dragon, Beelzebub, and the accuser of the brethren. The common thread in these roles is *violence*. 1 Peter 5:8 states: "Be sober, be vigilant; because your adversary the devil, as a roaring lion, walketh about, seeking whom he may devour."

This is reinforced in the book, *The Three Battlegrounds*, by Francis Frangipane, page 18, which states: "You will remember that, at the fall of man in the Garden of Eden, the judgment of God against the devil was that he should "eat dust." Remember also that God said of man, "dust thou art" (Gen. 3:14-19). The essence of our carnal nature—is dust. We need to see the connection here: Satan feeds upon our earthly, carnal nature of "dust."

Satan's appetite for the believers living for Christ is ferocious. We must stay diligent to identify his traps. As we continue to seek wholeness, the attacks from Satan will only increase. However, for the purposes of this book I will focus on three characteristics that Satan will manifest to attack and try to upend us within workplaces. His main characteristics are an accuser (faultfinder), deceiver (liar) and enticer.

Accuser of the Brethren

The Bible tells us a good name should be chosen over great wealth (Proverbs 3:12). Our parents instill in us to behave wisely because our name will precede us wherever we go. As an accuser, Satan's primary goal is to gain access to us so he can discredit us in the eyes of God. He seeks to destroy anyone who is living uprightly in the sight of God. The bible warns us that individuals living godly and with integrity unto Christ will suffer persecution (2 Timothy 3:12). As we briefly discussed in a previous chapter, Job, was a righteous and God-fearing man. God gave Satan permission to test Job. However, Satan's hypothesis was that Job only feared God because of the wealth and quality of life and hedge of protection God had placed around Job. However, God knew of Job's heart. Eventually, Job lost everything – including his health, but refused to curse God as Satan had asserted[22].

So, as Christians in the workplace, we will be tested, but it always works in our favor. There have been countless times when we have done everything according to the book on a project, but our work is still brought into question. In my case, I was accused of not doing my job, although I followed proper procedure. I documented my work and conversations with the client using email. The client told a blatant lie and said I never provided them with the steps needed to complete our process. At the time, I worked for a government

---

[22] Job 2:10 Kings James Version

agency, so the client (petitioner) was attempting to get approval for a project without following procedure. I was able to produce the email that documented the fact that I provided the details of the process for approval.

The key to success is not to take it personally. It is hard, but if you understand the source of the attack, you will be able to successfully endure your season of persecution. As Christians, you must know that regardless of where you are, home, work or church, Satan will persecute you. There is a season for everything, but being talked about, mistreated, ignored and the like is part of the game.

However, we cannot fight against the individual or person that Satan will use to fight against us. 2 Corinthians 10:3 states: "For though we walk in the flesh, we do not war according to the flesh" (NKJV). As Christians, our tools for battle are spiritual. We must learn to counteract Satan's attack in the spiritual realm and not in the natural realm. Jesus told the woman at the well that God seeks true worshippers to worship him in spirit and in truth. As Christians, we are now spiritual beings that have been regenerated by the Holy Spirit.

If we try to fight Satan in the natural realm, he wins because we must react out of our flesh by ignoring the leading of the Holy Spirit. It took me a while to realize that Satan was behind the attacks on my character and the mistreatment by co-workers, family members, and so-called friends. I grew tired of being upset all the time and replaying the attacks and vicious words over and over in my head.

One day I simply asked the Lord in prayer, "Is it me? What is it about me that people don't like?" He said, "It is not you; it is because of the God in you." That liberated my spirit, and I felt a weight lifted off me. Jesus told his disciples in John 15:18-17: "If the world hates you, ye know that it hated me before *it hated* you. If ye were of the world, the world would love its own: but because ye are not of the world, but I have chosen you out of the world, therefore the world hateth you."

As Christians, we are a chosen and unique set of people. Ephesians 1:4 states: "For he chose us in him [Jesus] before the creation of the world to be holy and blameless in his sight. In love..." (NIV). Once we have the Holy Spirit, which is the Spirit of God, we become a part of the Body of Christ and the natural enemy of Satan. So, it is his job and sole occupation to persecute us and ruin our names.

We are not left to our own devices to defend ourselves. Hold up your head and be encouraged because Romans 8:28 states: "And we know that all things work together for good to them that love God, to them who are the called according to *his* purpose." Every persecution, test, and tribulation only adds to the purpose that God has designed for our lives. Satan can bring accusations against us, but he does not have the power or authority over us unless God gives him permission to attack us. Yet, Satan has set-parameters that he cannot override.

For instance, Joshua, an Old Testament high priest, is an example; God tells Satan to keep his dirty paws off his chosen. Zechariah 3:1-2 states: "And he shewed me Joshua the high priest standing before the angel of the LORD and Satan standing at his right hand to resist him. And the LORD said unto Satan, The LORD rebuke thee, O Satan; even the LORD that hath chosen Jerusalem rebuke thee: *is* not this a brand plucked out of the fire?"

Joshua[23] had just come out of a difficult season in which he had failed. However, he did not try to hide himself, but presented himself unto the angel of the God. So Satan thought he could continue his persecution, but God said: *No, he has been through enough. I will forgive him of his iniquity and reward him for enduring the trial* (Zechariah 3:4-5).

In essence, we must endure the difficult seasons in our lives by knowing that God dictates when our season will end. If we endure, we will be honored by him for our perseverance and faith. Will we do everything right all the time? No. Nevertheless, if we are honest and keep our trust in God, then he will be faithful to us, just as he was to Joshua the high priest.

Satan the Ultimate Deceiver and Tempter

Satan is notoriously known as a deceiver and liar. He can also be classified as a tempter. Two watershed moments for Christians in the Bible include: the deception of Eve in the Garden of Eden and

---

[23] Son of Josedech Haggai 1:1

temptation of Christ in the wilderness. Genesis Chapter 3 sets the stage for Satan, disguised as a serpent, to convince Eve to eat of the Tree of Knowledge of Good and Evil.

God gave Adam, her husband, the initial commandment in Genesis 2:16-17, however, Satan did not waste any time to break up the honeymoon of Adam and Eve, since she was created at the end of Chapter 2. He wanted to come between God and Adam, but used Eve and the serpent to do so. He did not try to tempt Adam directly, because of Adam's authority and his direct relationship with God.

Satan is strategic in how he operates and always has a primary objective for his actions. Most times, with a few exceptions, he works through others to attack his target. First, he selected the most crafty and subtle creature in God's kingdom to manipulate (Genesis 3:1).

The serpent, for instance, was described as subtle and devious. He also played on the lack of Eve's understanding of God's commandment. He quizzed her first to determine what she understood about eating from the trees in the Garden. Satan never mentioned the Tree of Knowledge of Good and Evil, but allowed Eve to incorporate it into the conservation. She responded, as recorded in Genesis 3:3: "But of the fruit of the tree which *is* in the midst of the garden, God hath said, 'Ye shall not eat of it, neither shall ye touch it, lest ye die.'" Satan was subtle, but deliberately evil, as he told Eve that she would not die instantly from eating the fruit of the forbidden tree.

Satan was successful in his deception because he tapped into her desires and was able to draw her away from the truth (Genesis 3:5). He explained the benefits of eating from the tree, such as gaining wisdom and being like a god with the ability to know all. The Bible states in Genesis 3:6: "And when the woman saw that the tree *was* good for food, and that it *was* pleasant to the eyes, and a tree to be desired to make *one* wise, she took of the fruit thereof, and did eat, and gave also unto her husband with her, and he did eat."

As a deceiver and tempter, Satan tries to lure us away by what we lust after and desire. The process of temptation is explained in the book of James 1:14-15: "But every man is tempted, when he is drawn away of his own lust and enticed. Then when lust hath conceived, it bringeth forth sin: and sin, when it is finished, bringeth forth death." In the case of Eve, she did not die until the Process of Temptation™ was complete, since the penalty of death was not given until after she and her husband ate the forbidden fruit. Given the Process of Temptation, it is crucial for us to understand our triggers, weaknesses and desires. If we have areas in our lives that are centered on the lust of the eye, the lust of the flesh, and the pride of life, then we are leaving an open door for Satan to deceive and tempt us.

Summary

Satan transforms into several characters in his attempt to over throw us. Yet, we know God lifts up a standard against his actions.

Understanding his background gives us insight into the way he operates and the types of personalities used to manifest in our lives. Common characteristics in people that should give you pause include boastful, arrogant, cunning, duplicitous, selfish and self-centered. Satan cannot attack us directly. He must use a vessel who has the characteristics similar to him. Although I shared his background and motives in this chapter, I want you to ponder the type of people who have caused you pain in the past. Answer the following questions to help you build a profile of the personalities used in the workplace:

1. If you were sabotaged on a project, was it by a co-worker, supervisor or administrative staff?
2. Describe the individual's personality. Do they need to be in forefront all the time or do they work quietly behind the scenes?
3. If they are not in a role of authority, are they considered an influencer or support to individuals in authority?
4. Gender is not always consistent since men and women can be used to attack you. However, which gender did you encounter the most attacks from male, female or was it even?

If you worked for different employers but engaged with the same personality type list the characteristics each person had in common, i.e. liar, aggressive, negative, jealous, accusatory, etc.

Chapter Four

POWER TOOLS FOR WINNING

The key to winning, as I mentioned previously, is to fight Satan in the arena where we have the authority. As Christians, we are empowered by the Holy Spirit and must operate within the spiritual arena. We can no longer respond as we did before we were transformed with physical violence, vicious words, and passive-aggressive behavior.

Instead, our power tools for fighting Satan are through the righteousness of God. So, what exactly do I mean? The scripture 2 Corinthians 10:4 states: "The weapons we fight with are not the weapons of the world. On the contrary, they have divine power to demolish strongholds" (NIV). As Christians, we are privy to an entire force of supernatural tools and creatures, yes I said creatures, that we can activate to destroy the areas dominated by Satan and put him to an open shame.

The power tools that only Christians have at their disposal are explained in the book of Ephesians Chapter 6. However, at this point, I must give you a disclaimer. The power tools of God will only work for Christians, who have truly been transformed and are obedient to the Holy Ghost. In other words, don't expect God to move on your behalf when you are being disruptive in meetings, bullying your co-workers, and discrediting them behind their backs. In order for the power tools to be effective, you must have endured the purification process and have your spirit under subjection. God cannot work his righteousness through our anger (James 1:20).

The armor of God, which are power tools for winning, is introduced in Ephesians 6:10-13 as follows: "Finally, my brethren, be strong in the Lord, and in the power of his might. Put on the whole armor of God that ye may be able to stand against the wiles of the devil. For we wrestle not against flesh and blood, but against principalities, against powers, against the rulers of the darkness of this world, against spiritual wickedness in high *places*. Wherefore take unto you the whole armor of God that ye may be able to withstand in the evil day, and having done all, to stand."

Armor of God

In the ancient days, a coat of armor was constructed of strong metal, and it protected the solider who wore it. Typically, it covered the entire body. Likewise, the armor of God is described in Ephesians 6:14-20; it provides protection for every part of an individual except for his back. The chapter talks about the loins, breastplate, helmet, feet, shield, and a sword. In the natural sense, the armor would be incomplete when your arms, legs, and back are exposed.

However, we are in the spiritual realm, and the armor protects our spirit, which is the inner man. The spirit controls the mind, body, and ultimately the soul. As your spirit goes, so goes your soul. Job 32:8 states: "But *there is* a spirit in man; and the inspiration of the Almighty giveth them understanding." So, our spirit must be fully integrated with the Holy Spirit, which provides the armor of God through which we operate. I will provide a brief description of each component of the armor of God.

Truth

The Truth, which is the Word of God, is our compass, our sustenance and life force. We must use the Word of God to strengthen us in our core. Ephesians 10:14 states: "Stand therefore, having your loins girt about with truth." The Truth, who is Christ, empowers us to stand against any adversity that bombards us. He is the Way, the Truth and the Life (John 14:6). We have double insulation against the powers of darkness because the written Word guides us and the Truth lives in us.

Isaiah 59:19 states: "...When the enemy shall come in like a flood, the Spirit of the LORD shall lift up a standard against him."

Strategically located in the "loins," or core of our spirit, the Truth is the source of power that helps us move and resist Satan. Our actions must always be centered on the truth.

Breastplate of Righteousness – Shield for our Hearts

Living in obedience to the Word of God positions us to be acceptable to God. Acceptance leads to favor, which leads to authority. Obeying the commandments of God will allow us to be defenders of God. The scripture 2 Corinthians 10:6 states: "...And having a readiness to revenge all disobedience, when your obedience is fulfilled." Thus, we cannot be effective in fighting the disobedience of Satan if we have not first fulfilled our own obedience to God.

The breastplate of righteousness is in essence us doing what the Word of God says, in spite of how we feel. We must go against our own human nature and worldly wisdom in order to obey the commandments of God.

For instance, Jesus said in Matthew 6:43: "Ye have heard that it hath been said, thou shalt love thy neighbor, and hate thine enemy. But I say unto you, love your enemies, bless them that curse you, do good to them that hate you, and pray for them which despitefully use you, and persecute you; That ye may be the children of your Father which is in heaven: for he maketh his sun to rise on the evil and on the good, and sendeth rain on the just and on the unjust." Our righteousness must exceed that of religious leaders that are focused on tradition and adherence to laws, without addressing the underlining motivation (Matthew 5:20).

This is a hard commandment for many of us, but through prayer and submission to the Holy Ghost we can be obedient to his Word regardless of how we are treated. Obedience to the Word of God keeps our hearts pure and free of unforgiveness and bitterness. Jesus also taught us in Matthew 6:14-15: "For if ye forgive men their trespasses, your heavenly Father will also forgive you: But if ye forgive not men their trespasses, neither will your Father forgive your trespasses." Forgiveness is key to our own deliverance and forgiveness for our sins. We already know that if we confess our sins, God is faithful to forgive us and cleanse us from all unrighteousness. So, maintaining a forgiving spirit will also keep our hearts pure.

Girdle of Truth – Strengthens our Core

Righteousness is a product of truth because if you have the truth, then you can live righteously. Proverbs 12:17 states: "He that speaketh truth sheweth forth righteousness; but a false witness speaks deceit." We must also take notice that the "girdle of truth" protects our loins, which includes our lower stomach and upper thighs. This region of our body is known in the natural realm as "the powerhouse" of our body. Any movements in our body must originate from this region, so it is important that we are reinforced and strengthened in that area.

Conversely, in the spiritual realm our loins must be reinforced with truth. Our movements in the spirit must originate from the truth. Psalms 119:142 states: "Thy righteousness is an everlasting righteousness, and thy law is the truth." *Strong's Hebrew Lexicon* defines truth as *stability and continuance*. So, truth will give us balance, and it will strengthen us so that we may continue in our walk with the Lord.

Feet Shod with the Preparation of the Gospel of Peace — Be a Peacemaker

We are to first seek peace with everyone, believers or non-believers. We are commanded to be peacemakers since we cannot fight our own battles. One of the traits of a Christian is peace. If we're truly women of faith, then we can't be full of drama and the source of strife and division among our co-workers. Jesus taught his disciples in Matthew 5:9: "Blessed *are* the peacemakers: for they shall be called the children of God." We can't be a credible example if we are constantly causing confusion. I Corinthians 14:33 states: "For God is not the author of confusion, but of peace, as in all churches of the saints."

As we walk with Christ, we must be peacemakers because He is the Prince of Peace. He gives us peace. We have to follow the path of peace in everything we do. As working women and leaders in the marketplace, a peacemaker is valuable to the company. In essence you build relationships and strategic partnerships. Everyone knows the "hell raiser" in the company that no one wants to work with. Winners set the atmosphere for excellence and productivity.

Lastly, Hebrews 12:14-15 states: "Follow peace with all *men* and holiness, without which no man shall see the Lord, looking diligently lest any man fail of the grace of God; lest any root of bitterness springing up trouble *you*, and thereby many be defiled."

Shield of Faith - Faith Quenches Satan's Attack

Faith in one's self in the workplace is major. If you lack faith in yourself, then others will not have faith in you. Working women must have faith to be successful. Many times, we may be the only woman in the room. Other times, we have to have the faith to get the job done because there are times we don't know how the project will be completed, but the job gets done.

The Bible defines faith as, "...the substance of things hoped for and the evidence of things not seen" (Hebrews 11:1). In Ephesians 6:14, the Greek word for faith is defined as fidelity or faithfulness, which means "the character of one who can be relied on." Thus, faith means to hope for something or someone that is unseen, who is both faithful and reliable.

That is an awesome thought—that we have our confidence and trust in a God we have not seen, yet we know he is faithful and reliable. That is why the writer said in Psalms 84:11: "For the Lord God is a sun and shield; the Lord will give grace and glory; no good thing will he withhold from them that walk uprightly."

For instance, Jesus told his disciples in Mark 11:22: ". . . Have faith in God." Jesus went on to explain the benefit of faith in Mark

11:23: "For verily I say unto you, that whosoever shall say unto this mountain, 'Be thou removed, and be thou cast into the sea;' and shall not doubt in his heart, but shall believe that those things which he saith shall come to pass; he shall have whatsoever he saith." Again, in Mark 9:23, Jesus said to a man seeking healing for his daughter: ". . . If thou canst believe, all things are possible to him that believeth."

Simply believing in God through the name of Jesus Christ will not only give us good things as mentioned in Psalms 84:11, but will also empower us to help someone else. Let's look at the work of faith wrought by Peter and John in third chapter of Acts. It is a familiar story of the lame man who was seeking alms of the people at the gate called Beautiful before the temple. As Peter and John walked up the steps of the porch to the temple, the man asked for a handout.

However, Acts 3:4-5 states: "And Peter fastening his eyes upon him with John, said, 'Look on us.' And he gave heed unto them, expecting to receive something of them." We must take note of something very important in this text. The Bible says that the man expected something. That is faith in action, because he had to believe they were going to give him something. So, if we want to receive something from God, we must first expect that He will give it to us. With an expectation, there is no room for doubt. If we know that we will receive it, then it becomes a matter of when he will give it to us. In other words, we will anticipate and look forward to receiving what we asked.

Basically, the man's faith in God through the name of Jesus Christ made him whole. Our faith in God, through Jesus Christ will make us whole, complete, and lacking for nothing. Similarly, our faith will be a shield unto us, like the one described in Ephesians 6:14. The Greek word thureos {thoo-re-hos} describes this type of shield as a long and oblong-shaped shield with four corners like a door. In this context, the shield will not only provide protection, but will also give access to resources and riches in the Kingdom of God.

Helmet of Salvation

The protection of our minds is of the utmost importance in our fight against the whiles of the devil. Proverbs 23:7a states: "As a man thinketh in his heart so is he . . ." We must guard our thoughts and be disciplined in our thinking as we encounter adversity in the workplace. Satan comes to kill, steal and destroy our confidence in God. He wants to destroy the very essence of who God has ordained us to be. The Helmet of Salvation shields our thoughts and imaginations to think on the things of God that will uplift us in times of trouble.

The hope of being rescued by God gives us confidence and protects us from desolation. The helmet of salvation represents us having the "presence of mind" to trust in God's ability to deliver us from our current situation, as well as in the future.

The natural propensity of our minds is to be pessimistic. On the other hand, we need some negativity to warn us of impending dangers. However, we cannot allow it to be a paralyzing force, which would hinder us from being irrepressible.

Isaiah 26:3 says it best: "You will keep him in perfect peace, whose mind is stayed on you, because he trusts in you" (NKJV). Our reliance in God fortifies our thought process to receive his direction even while we are under siege. As believers, we must rewire our minds to be optimistic regardless of the circumstance. The helmet protects us from being insecure and provides stability during distressing times.

Sometimes our natural mind is discouraged and uneasy about our circumstances. In addition, the devil is bombarding our minds with fiery darts of fear and doubt at the same time. Thus, if we put on the "hope of salvation" as a helmet, then we will be able to rely on God regardless of the situation. We will also be able to praise Him in advance for the victory and deliverance that will come.

The Helmet of Salvation protects our minds and thoughts so that we can focus on Jesus instead of on our problems. As stated in 2 Corinthians 10:5: "Casting down imaginations and every high thing that exalteth itself against the knowledge of God and bringing into captivity every thought to the obedience of Christ." Hope will also allow us to praise and rejoice in Jesus Christ when we are at our lowest point emotionally and spiritually.

Sword of Spirit

Last but not least, the Sword of the Spirit, which is the Word of God, is our weapon to defeat Satan. In the marketplace, we must be knowledgeable and assertive in order to be productive. We use our command of the industry language and experience to address any challenge to our competence. However, we'll face occasions when we need the Word of God to go before us and solidify our success.

As the founder and finisher of our faith, Jesus Christ is the Word of God (Hebrews 12:2). A vivid description of Jesus is given by the Apostle John in Revelations 19:13-15:

> 13: And he was clothed with a vesture dipped in blood: and his name is called The Word of God.
> 14: And the armies which were in heaven followed him upon white horses, clothed in fine linen, white and clean.
> 15: And out of his mouth goeth a sharp sword, that with it he should smite the nations: and he shall rule them with a rod of iron: and he treadeth the winepress of the fierceness and wrath of Almighty God.

Jesus is our ultimate weapon because of his obedience to the will of God, which was death on the cross at Calvary. Upon the fulfillment of his duty to reconcile the creation of mankind back to

God he was given all power (Hebrews 1:2-3). As a result, he is the King of Kings and Lord of Lords.

As our defender, Jesus will go before us in our trials to give us the victory just as he did for Joshua in the battle of Jericho. The bible states in Joshua 6:2, "And the LORD said unto Joshua, 'See, I have given into thine hand Jericho, and the king thereof, and the mighty men of valor.'" Yes, they had to follow specific instructions including walking around the large gated city in silence for six days, and they were only allowed to shout on the seventh day (Joshua 6:1-27).

In spite of this, the victory was already secured because Jesus Christ led the charge as the captain of the Lord's army before anyone took one step around the wall. Most accounts of the story fail to mention the encounter that Joshua had with Jesus. The encountered is captured in Joshua 5:13-15:

> "13: And it came to pass, when Joshua was by Jericho, that he lifted up his eyes and looked, and behold, there stood a man over against him with his sword drawn in his hand: and Joshua went unto him, and said unto him, Art thou for us, or for our adversaries?
> 14: And he said, Nay; but as captain of the host of the LORD am I now come. And Joshua fell on his face to the earth,

and did worship, and said unto him,
What saith my lord unto his servant?

15: And the captain of the LORD'S
host said unto Joshua, loose thy shoe
from off thy foot; for the place,
whereon thou standest is holy. And
Joshua did so."

Yes, it can be argued that Jesus was not yet born because Israel was not established as an official nation. Others have stated that Joshua saw an angel. However, angels, who are ministering spirits, are not to be worshipped, only the Lord God (Exodus 34:14). Worshipping anyone or thing other than God was breaking the first commandment, which is a mistake Joshua would not make. He was faithful and full of integrity as a leader among his people.

In addition, King David[24] was given the revelation of Jesus as Lord in Psalms 110:1, which states: "The LORD said unto my Lord, sit thou at my right hand, until I make thine enemies thy footstool." Jesus also testified of his authority in John 8:57-58, "Then said the Jews unto him, 'Thou art not yet fifty years old, and hast thou seen Abraham?' Jesus said unto them, 'Verily, verily, I say unto you, Before Abraham[25] was, I am.'"

Likewise, as we face the defining moments in our lives, we can experience the manifestation of the presence of Jesus Christ. Our

---

[24] David king over all Israel (2Sa 5:1-5; 1Ch 11:1-3)
[25] Smith's Bible Dictionary - (father of a multitude) was the son of Terah, and founder of the great Hebrew nation. (B.C. 1996-1822)

love and fulfillment of his commandments provide an opportunity for us to experience the miraculous. Joshua set out to achieve the impossible by overtaking a walled city without the use of weapons because of his continued faith in the spoken Word of God, which led to the manifestation of the living Word of God. It is God's desire to manifest his presence in our lives and to defend us. All we must do is believe in him and his Word.

The Bible states in Hebrews 11:1, "Now, faith is the substance of things hoped for, the evidence of things not seen." Although we cannot see the end result, we must take God at his word and believe that what he has spoken will manifest.

In the fall of 2013, my 76-year-old mother was diagnosed with Endometrial Cancer, a disease in which malignant (cancer) cells form in the tissues of the endometrium (or uterus lining). I had recently started a new job, but God gave me favor with my supervisor to work from home and use flexible time to take my mom to the doctor. I was able to get all the testing complete that verified my Mom had cancer. We scheduled all of her treatments, including the necessary surgery, but a few weeks prior to the surgery she cancelled it. She refused to get any treatment. Of course, I conferred with the nurses and relatives who were in the medical field, but there was nothing I could do because it was her decision. She was capable of taking care of herself, so the decision was in her hands.

As her only daughter I was devastated. I cried out to God, asking him what to do. I was dumbfounded. I had that spirit of heaviness and was mourning. Talk about a test of my faith. My mom told me, "If God allows me to die, then so be it." Well, I could not take any comfort in those words. I will never forget the night I was driving home from work. All of these thoughts and words from the doctors and nurses swirled in my spirit, "It is aggressive and must be treated." Suddenly, I heard clearly within my spirit, "It's not what the doctors say; it's what I say. I have the last word." I immediately felt the power of God fill that car, and I began to cry out in relief. I cried and thanked God for his Word. The Bible states in Isaiah 53:5b, "...the chastisement of our peace was upon him; and with his stripes we are healed."

From that point on I went to battle in the prayer for my mother's healing. I know she was praying, and at times, we prayed together. However, I stood battle-ready to take on the big "C." Yes, it was difficult as I watched my mother lose weight and her hair thin and break-off. Despite what I saw on the outward appearance, I believed God for her healing.

Fast forward to the fall of 2014, almost a year later, and my mother was sick, so she finally agreed to go to the hospital. I informed them that she was diagnosed with cancer a year ago, and they ran some tests. I remember one nurse said to me, "She looks good to have cancer." Ultimately, she was cleared of cancer. Hallelujah, all praise to God! Our prayers were answered. His word will defend you in the face of adversity.

Summary

The armor of God is the arsenal we need to defend ourselves against Satan. Yet, the tools are rendered powerless if our heart is full of bitterness and wrath. Our obedience to the written word of God activates the source to generate supernatural power through the Holy Spirit. Our lifestyle must align with God to become vessels used to avenge his word. Faith is the common denominator as we place our confidence in God's ability to help us. However, showing love to the individuals who despise us protects our spirit from bitterness. Components such peace, truth, and righteousness are polar opposites to characteristics of Satan identified in the previous chapter. We must seek to be like Christ, if we expect to have the authority to thrive in the face of adversity. Using the same tactics as Satan will only frustrate us and ruin our integrity as Christians. Answer the following questions regarding the characteristics of Christ:

1. List 2 actions that demonstrate the breastplate of righteousness?
2. Write down 1 event when you used the shield of Faith?
3. Provide an example of being a peacemaker?
4. Describe a situation when the truth strengthens you to prevail over an accuser?
5. Write down the names of your accusers, attackers, adversaries on your job in a journal and pray for them.

Chapter Five

EFFECTIVE COMMUNICATION

Effective communication begins with confidence. As working women, we know that confidence is fundamental to being respected in our areas of expertise. As Christians, our confidence must be in God to obtain the results we seek. Godly confidence is greatly rewarded. Hebrews 10:35 states: "So do not throw away your confidence; it will be richly rewarded" (NIV).

Jesus also taught that unwavering faith produces great results. Jesus said in John 14:14: "If ye shall ask any thing in my name, I will do *it*." However, the beginning of that chapter explicitly states that we must believe in Him. As we have discussed above, faith in God unlocks unlimited possibilities.

In this final chapter, I want to convey the importance of faith and communication. Many times, the world mocks Christians and mimics our sayings, such as "I'm blessed and highly favored" or "Speak it and receive it." Well, the power of faith and communication are real. As I mentioned earlier, we have the God-given authority to speak to situations to bring about a change.

On the other hand, effective communication begins with a lifestyle and a routine. Our lifestyle determines how intimately we can interact with God. It is difficult to be in a relationship with individuals that do not share the same lifestyle that we embrace. In addition, when we are in a relationship with an individual, we want to speak to them all the time. Likewise, our lives must align with the directives of God, so that we may engage with him on a regular basis.

The passage 1 John 5:3-4 states: "In fact, this is love for God: to keep his commands. And his commands are not burdensome, for everyone born of God overcomes the world, even on faith" (NIV). As we spend more personal time with God, we learn his language and position ourselves to become winners, because our lifestyle is transformed by his love.

For instance, being a mentee of a CEO (Chief Executive Officer) from a major corporation would give us access to their knowledge base. As a mentor, the individual would share their life lessons and insights on running a company. Similarly, living a God-centered lifestyle gives us access to the greatest mentor of all. We hear how to overcome the obstacles placed in our paths while praying for the individuals who oppose us (Matthew 5:44).

Furthermore, the relationship is solidified with regularly scheduled talks. A good relationship of any type requires individuals to talk to each other. So, a solid relationship with God requires us to talk with him on a daily basis, instead of only when we need something.

Case in point, I set a daily appointment time to spend with God and to pray. I started with 10 minutes. I used my drive time to work because I was alone and most times, traffic was at a snail's pace. Over the course of a week, I saw results immediately. My demeanor changed, and I was no longer uptight and stressed out. I learned to remain calm under pressure instead of blowing my top like a teapot ready to spew hot water.

Soon, I began to wake up a few minutes earlier to pray while my family was asleep. I just enjoyed the intimacy with God and learned to love him outside of the four walls of a religious institution. My belief is that God reserves a place within each of us that only he can occupy. We merely need to open our hearts and minds to receive the love and wisdom God so desperately wants to share.

Conversely, the honeymoon did not last forever. I was soon put to the test with additional adversity on my job. Dealing with bullies in the workplace was exasperating. I learned to look inward and improve myself instead of being a victim. As I mentioned in

Chapter 1, I completed a personal SWOT analysis to eliminate any areas that would give him easy access for an attack.

My faith was fortified through my personal relationship with God. I was prepared like a champion boxer for the major title fight. I was ready to go against Satan toe to toe, instead of being ambushed like a sitting duck, unaware of my surroundings.

I learned to recognize the force working behind the individuals and not retaliate against them. God showed me how to pray for the individuals, who sabotaged my work and hurled insults at me in front of others. Prayer was my tool to speak to God about the conditions and ask him to change it on my behalf. **Matthew 6:6 states: "But thou, when thou prayest, enter into thy closet, and when thou hast shut thy door, pray to thy Father which is in secret; and thy Father which seeth in secret shall reward thee openly" (KJV).** My secret prayer made a positive impact on any situation I faced. Later in the chapter I will discuss a few of the methods I used to change situations through prayer.

Soon, other coworkers noticed the change in my demeanor. A few of the individuals who'd initially bullied me, asked me to pray with them. One individual in particular was stricken with a disease. The person was cured of one medical condition, but other health problems emerged. I was in my office one afternoon, and the individual stepped inside, closed the door and said, "Do you have a minute? I want you to pray for me. I have to go back to the doctor and get some additional tests." I nodded and stood so we could pray for a positive report from the doctor. A few weeks later I received the good news that everything checked out to be fine.

The life of an efficacious believer comes from being broken in spirit from the various challenges we face. If we are confident in our own abilities without the help of God, then he cannot operate through us. Rather, we must become humble to enable the power and authority of the Holy Spirit to freely flow through our lives. God will reveal his plan of action when we acquiesce to Him.

James 4:6 states: "But he giveth more grace. Wherefore he saith, God resisteth the proud, but giveth grace unto the humble." The act of humility entails a makeover of our lives from what we know. Enduring the bullying, trials and temptations that come to try our faith is a basic requirement.

God will honor our prayers when we have a lifestyle to affirm them. Hebrews 13:16 states: "But to do good and to communicate forget not: for with such sacrifices God is well pleased." This also brings to mind of the story of Cornelius[26] in the New Testament.

After the crucifixion, resurrection and ascension of Jesus Christ, the promise of the Comforter, the Holy Ghost was soon to come. The establishment of the New Testament Church occurred on the day of Pentecost[27] when 120 men and women, including the 11

---

[26] Cornelius, the first Gentile convert to Christianity, was a Centurion, a Roman officer in command of a hundred men. Easton's Bible Dictionary

[27] The day of Pentecost is noted in the Christian Church as the day on which the Spirit descended upon the apostles, and on which, under Peter's preaching, so many thousands were converted in Jerusalem (Act 2). Easton's Bible Dictionary

apostles and Mary the mother of Jesus, were filled with the Holy Ghost. They were all Jews, because Jesus Christ ministered to the descendants of the nation of Israel. Acts 2:36 states: "Therefore let all the house of Israel know assuredly, that God hath made that same Jesus, whom ye have crucified, both Lord and Christ." So, it was known that the salvation of God was unto the Jews first. However, God's grand plan was for all mankind, Jew and Gentile (non-Jewish) to be reconciled unto him and have salvation through Jesus Christ. Romans 2:11 states: "For there is no respect of persons with God."

Now enters Cornelius, a Gentile and leader in the Roman army who lived uprightly before God (Acts 10:1). Although his lifestyle and prayers gained God's attention, Cornelius did not know the plan of salvation to become a Christian. God sent his angel to tell Cornelius how to learn about being a Christian. Acts 10: 4-6 states:

> 4: And when he [Cornelius] looked on him [the angel], he was afraid, and said, 'What is it, Lord?' And he [the angel] said unto him [Cornelius], 'Thy prayers and thine alms are come up for a memorial before God.
>
> 5: And now send men to Joppa, and call for one Simon, whose surname is Peter:
>
> 6: He lodgeth with one Simon a tanner, whose house is by the sea side: he shall tell thee what thou oughtest to do.'

Although Cornelius was obedient, God also dealt with Peter, because in the Jewish culture, Jews and Gentiles did not associate unless the Gentile was converted (Acts 10:28). This was a milestone for the New Testament Church and a test for Peter because he had to realize that God's salvation was for everyone. During his routine prayer time, God dealt with Peter in a vision. Acts 10:11-15 states:

> 11: And [Peter] saw heaven opened, and a certain vessel descending unto him, as it had been a great sheet knit at the four corners, and let down to the earth:
>
> 12: Wherein were all manner of four-footed beasts of the earth, and wild beasts, and creeping things, and fowls of the air.
>
> 13: And there came a voice to him, 'Rise, Peter; kill, and eat.'
>
> 14: But Peter said, 'Not so, Lord; for I have never eaten anything that is common or unclean.'
>
> 15: And the voice spake unto him again the second time, 'What God hath cleansed, that call not thou common.'

Although Peter did not fully understand the vision, the Holy Spirit continued to direct him and let him know that the men Cornelius sent were looking for him, and it was safe for him to follow them.

Peter was obedient and did as the Spirit led him. I found it interesting that God didn't reveal the entire plan to Peter until after he went to Cornelius's home and met him in person.

Cornelius was able to tell Peter of his vision and how he was told to find him so he could be told what to do. It was at that point that Peter realized the entire plan of God's salvation as he stated in Acts 10:34-36, "Then Peter opened his mouth, and said, of a truth I perceive that God is no respecter of persons: But in every nation, he that feareth him, and worketh righteousness, is accepted with him. The word which God sent unto the children of Israel, preaching peace by Jesus Christ: (he is Lord of all)."

Consequentially, Peter preached the gospel of Jesus Christ and all the works of his life including his resurrection and ascension into heaven. As he was still speaking, everyone listening received the Holy Ghost and began to speak in tongues. It amazed the Jews who had come with Peter because until that moment, only the Jews had received salvation. In summary, if we live a life with integrity before God, he will honor us and connect us to the right people. God brought two people together by the leading of the Holy Spirit and implemented his master plan of salvation for everyone by the hand of a man who lived righteously before him.

Communication to God is more than spewing out your wish list and complaints about your co-workers, employees or supervisors. Communication with God is about a relationship and taking the time to commune with him. As we live through Christ, we take on his characteristics and can perform the same miracles and works of faith that he did while on earth. Jesus stated in John 14:12: "Verily, verily, I say unto you, he that believeth on me, the works that I do shall he do also; and greater works than these shall he do; because I go unto my Father." We all know that faith in God without works is unproductive. It is God's desire that we demonstrate his power and have a direct impact on our environments.

In terms of building a relationship, the Song of Solomon is such a wonderful description of the type of relationship we can have with God through Jesus Christ. The body of believers, referred to as the Bride or Body of Christ in the New Testament, is the symbol of the princess fawning after her King (Song of Solomon 7:10). It is a spiritual allegory[28] of the personal relationship that as individuals and as the corporate body of believers, we can have with our Creator.

Many in religious institutions place God on the throne high above the universe in the heavens. However, I am here to give you my personal testimony that we serve a God and King who is ever-present in our lives. The three persons of the Godhead (1 John 5:8) will come right to where we are to comfort and love us and to fellowship with us.

I have personally experienced the presence of God in my times of despair. I have felt the healing power of the Holy Spirit saturate my body when I prayed to Christ for healing. On the other hand, I have experienced the joy and peace he brings in times of sweet devotions. I have sung songs of worship and admiration while worshipping at the foot of this throne.

---

[28] Chuck Smith C2000 Series on Song of Solomon – BlueletterBible.com

Jesus told his disciples in John 14:23: "If a man love me, he will keep my words, and my Father will love him, and we will come unto him, and make our abode with him." Based on our love and the way we communicate that love, we have unlimited access to our God and King – Jesus Christ. Since we are beloved of God and belong to him we can make our requests known to him. Hebrews 4:6 states: "Let us therefore come boldly unto the throne of grace that we may obtain mercy and find grace to help in time of need."

We can communicate with God when we are in need and when we just want to spend quality time. Since we are one with him, we have the ability to live in his presence continually regardless of where we are or what we are doing. Watchman Nee reinforces this notion in his book, [29]*The Release of the Spirit*, which states: "When the outward man is broken, things outside will be kept outside, and the inward man will live continuously before God." Below I will share three types of communication, along with tips on being effective.

Fellowship – Lifestyle vs. Religious Ritual

Personal fellowship with God can occur outside of the four walls of a church. We should fellowship with God on a daily basis. As Christians, our bodies have become the tabernacle of the Spirit of God (1 Corinthian 3:16). In essence we are continually plugged into

---

[29] *The Breaking of the Outward Man for the Release of the Spirit*, Watchman Nee, 2000, Christian Fellowship Publication, Inc., Chapter 2, pg. 32

the wisdom, power, peace, and authority that have been established through Jesus Christ (Hebrews 10:20).

The digital age requires us to be constantly connected to current events, email, social media and the like. We are useless without our smart phones, because we must be constantly connected to know what is occurring on our jobs, with our friends and our families. Likewise, as Christians in the marketplace, we must be fully integrated and merged with Christ through the Holy Spirit, who is our comforter.

Jesus consoled his disciples in John 14:26: "But the Comforter, *who is* the Holy Ghost, whom the Father will send in my name, he shall teach you all things, and bring all things to your remembrance, whatsoever I have said unto you." A lifestyle of fellowship will keep us in the continual flow of the Holy Spirit. We will receive our instructions, warnings, and positive reinforcement on a continual basis.

Communing with God on a continual basis starts with prayer. If you do not pray on a regular basis, don't beat yourself up about it because it will lead to self-condemnation. This is just another trick of the enemy to keep your focus on negative thoughts instead of on Christ.

As we discussed in the prior chapter, condemnation is a mechanism used by our adversary to suppress our spirits and separate us from the peace, love and fellowship of God. Again, Romans 8:1 states: "There is therefore now no condemnation to them which are in Christ Jesus, who walk not after the flesh, but after the Spirit."

We all have areas in our lives that need improving. We must be honest with ourselves and submit our wills to him. Jesus was displeased with religious leaders who made long prayers in public, but were insincere (Mark 12:40). He would rather we pray a simple and private prayer directed to God. He states in Matthew 6:5: "And when thou prayest, thou shalt not be as the hypocrites are: for they love to pray standing in the synagogues and in the corners of the streets, that they may be seen of men. Verily I say unto you; they have their reward" (Matthew 6:6). When we pray in secret to God, we will be rewarded publicly.

The Ten-Minute Prayer

This is merely a starting point for women who feel they are too busy to pray for an hour. The trick is to schedule prayer the way you schedule your staff meetings or "standing appointments" with important clients. Block off 10 -15 minutes a day when you will not be distracted or interrupted to pray and fellowship with God.

I started during my commute to work. It was over 20 minutes of uninterrupted time that I could devote to prayer instead of listening to the radio or talking on my cell phone. I began to see the results immediately within my spirit. I was calmer and more focused when I arrived at work. It also put me in a wonderful mood, and I sang from the parking garage to the building.

It is an awesome way to start your day. In addition, I have received warnings or reminders to do things. The beauty of fellowship is that it is interactive. You send your songs and worship to God, and in turn, he gives you peace, joy, and wisdom.

Soon, the ten-minute prayer turned into the thirty minutes in the morning before I jumped into the shower. Being in the presence of God became so addictive I had to spend more time in his presence. The goal is to be in constant communication with God, walking in the Spirit as opposed to us going it alone.

As a result, fellowship becomes a part of your daily life and routine. Your mindset changes because you are in prayer mode continually. Within your mind you use your thoughts to access the power of the Holy Spirit. It becomes your first point of reference, instead of your own intellect. The old folks would say, "You being led by the Spirit, baby." Fellowship is a mindset and way of life that I cannot live without.

Just as physically fit women always work-out by taking the stairs, walking fast and jogging lightly through the office, we must exercise our spirits by communicating with God through the Holy Ghost on a consistent basis.

30-Minute Prayer

Prayer, just like exercise, is effective when you are consistent. Avid joggers are committed to running their three-to-five miles regardless of the weather conditions. I have seen women jogging in winter, and I think to myself, "Wow she is totally committed to running." As Christians, we must have the same level of commitment in our prayer life. Regardless of the way we feel – tired, upset or just lazy, we must commit to see Christ every day.

As I researched the Scriptures and learned from other Christians, effective prayer has a format. The Holy Spirit initially led me through the steps of prayer and the protocol to worship Christ. Upon further research, attending retreats and the like, I developed my own format that I follow to this day.

1. The Blood of Jesus – Pray in the name of Jesus Christ by applying the blood of Jesus Christ over yourself, your family, your home by stating: "I plead the blood of Jesus Christ over me, to cleanse me from all sins and to purify my spirit and mind from ungodliness.

2. Thanksgiving – Give Christ an offering of thanksgiving, by thanking Him for what He has already done and will continue to do in your life.

3. Repentance – Forgive those who have offended you and repent for the things you've done (knowingly and unknowingly).

4. Praise – Start with a song and sing it unto Christ with sincerity and joy.

5. Worship – Bless Christ with the fruit of your lips and a sincere heart. Revere and give honor unto his name just for being who He is, our Savior and King, and not for what he will do for you.

6. Request – Make your requests and petitions known before him. Seek to do his will, and pray for others before praying for yourself.

It is important to note that the actual prayer request is last. I became so intoxicated with the presence of Christ by worshiping him first that I would not even make a request. I just wanted to spend time with him and love on him and allow him to love me.

Psalms 96:7-9 explains it as follows: "Honor and majesty *are* before him: strength and beauty *are* in his sanctuary. Give unto the LORD the glory *due unto* his Name; bring an offering, and come into his courts. O worship the LORD in the beauty of holiness; fear before him, all the earth."

Praying in this format proved to be life-changing and efficacious. The fellowship and presence that I longed for was finally realized. I had the power to overcome the infirmities and issues that had nagged at my spirit for so many years. The hurt and abuse that seemed to knock me off my feet no longer had an effect on my spirit or thought process. I was able to simply shake things off and move forward in my spiritual walk with Christ. However, I reached a milestone in my prayer life where I felt as though I was not only standing in the presence of Christ, but in a place, that was outside of the limitations from any physical building or structure. I felt as though I were standing in a heavenly place.

Effective communication will put you at the origin of power, which is the Throne of God. In the workplace, communication is the vehicle to put you before decision makers, such as human resource directors, supervisors, managers and, yes, the Chief Executive Officer. Sincere and consistent prayer will place you at the feet of Jesus Christ. He is our advocate and appeals to God on our behalf when we are in need. Hebrews 9:24: "For Christ has not entered into the holy places made with hands, which are the figures of the true; but into heaven itself, now to appear in the presence of God for us...."

Positive Command

The second type of communication is to make a command. Working women know that if you want something, you must speak your mind and speak clearly and concisely. Timing is also important, but we must learn to speak with authority if we will be taken seriously. Your co-workers or employees will not take you seriously if you talk in circles without getting to your point. Most times you will be ignored during meetings.

Likewise, we have authority to speak what we need done by God, and he will move on our behalf. Of course, it is conditioned by the fact that we are in the divine will of God and believe that he will perform it. Jesus taught his disciples in John 5:7: "If ye abide in me, and my words abide in you, ye shall ask what ye will, and it shall be done unto you."

However, the breaking down of our outer man or spirit will enable God to work through our spirits without interference. Jesus stated in John 12:24: "He that loveth his life shall lose it; and he that hateth his life in this world shall keep it unto life eternal." Likewise, [30]*The Release of the Spirit, by Watchman Nee* states: "If the outward man remains unbroken, we can never be a blessing to his Church. And we cannot expect the Lord to bless the Word of God through us!"

In essence we become one with Christ because our hard-outer shells of the life we once loved are melted away, and our spirits are free to converge with Christ through the Holy Spirit.

Apostles Peter and John healed a man with a command. Acts 3:6-7 states: "Then Peter said, 'Silver and gold have I none; but such as I have I give thee: In the name of Jesus Christ of Nazareth rise up and walk.' And he took him by the right hand, and lifted him up: and immediately his feet and ankle bones received strength."
It was Peter and John's faith in the name of Jesus Christ to speak it, knowing that God would perform what they had asked. We, too, have the power to make commands that will change our situations.

There have been dozens of times when I was expecting a financial increase that was being delayed. I learned through my relationship with God, that I could command my funds to be released immediately. I was expecting the payout of some funds, and I knew that my wait was being prolonged. During my prayer time, I commanded that my funds be released immediately and dispatched my angels to retrieve them in the Name of Jesus. The

---

[30] *The Breaking of the Outward Man for the Release of the Spirit*, Watchman Nee, 2000, Christian Fellowship Publishers, Inc. Chapter 1 pg. 14

next week, I received a call telling me to come and pick up a check. This is not fiction or witchcraft, but we have the power of authority in our mouths to change our circumstances.

As Christians, we have angels that are given charge over us. They are at our disposal as long as we are in the will of God. The bible states in Psalms 34:7: "The angel of the LORD encampeth round about them that fear him, and delivereth them." Christians have resources and authority that have been given to us by the Holy Spirit. If we are in the mindset of fellowship, we can be directed what to say to change the situation.

Summary

We connect to God through our prayers. It is his desire to hear from us all the time. His attentive to us and seeks to hear our prayers. As I mentioned in Chapter 1, I began with short periods of prayer and increased over time. The longer you become intimate with God in your personal time, you begin to see a difference in your temperament, productivity and relationships with others. Our prayer time is a sacred place, shut off from the prying ears and eyes of our enemy Satan. We can boldly approach our father, God and make a request when we have a relationship with him. He is eager to grant it because he knows us and will not withhold any pleasant thing from us. Prayer integrates our spirit with his spirit, through the Holy Ghost. Once connected, we have a continuous source of power that strengthens us even when we are feeble.

1. Name an instance when you were unable to prayer, but you felt the power of Holy Spirit intercede for you.
2. Take out your personal schedule and lock in at 10 minutes of prayer every day for one week. Write down in your journal every day how you felt after your 10-minute power prayer.
3. During your prayer times, ask the Lord for a scripture and write down the passage in your journal.
4. Select two problems someone else is experiencing and pray them instead of yourself for a week. Make a note of when God answered the prayer.
5. During the same time period, did God solve any of your problems without you praying for help?

Conclusion

Living through the experience of workplace bullying has opened my spirit to receive the peace, wisdom and resilience that are available to us through the power of Holy Ghost. It is always daunting to go through hardship and ridicule, but once we have overcome, the victory is sweet.

My hardship over the course of my career prepared my heart to be more compassionate and patient with believers and non-believers. I had to become more mature as a Christian and realize that God wanted me to help individuals who didn't realize they needed help. The passage 2 Timothy 2:25-26 states: "...In meekness instructing those that oppose themselves; if God peradventure will give them repentance to the acknowledging of the truth; And that they may recover themselves out of the snare of the devil, who are taken captive by him at his will."

This guide has provided a game plan for us to be winners in the world, while maintaining our integrity and godliness. Oftentimes, women feel pressured to behave as the world puts it, "Like a Man," who is arrogant and heartless in order to get ahead. We don't have to take on the attitude and spirit of our bullies.

It is behavior that not all men engage in to be successful. A Christian woman should be able to exude the grace and sophistication that God has given her. A woman with a positive disposition and laid-back spirit will be just as successful as the over-aggressive and argumentative one. Christian working women are making strides and breaking down barriers like never before. It is okay to be godly and have standards. Understanding the traps of Satan will enable you to spot him from a mile away and detour the drama. It is equally important to know yourself so that you may grow as a Christian and produce more fruit unto the glory of God.

Positioned for Power

31-Day Prayer Journal

Prayers to strengthen your
spirit, give you wisdom, &
clarity to be a change agent
for Christ.

Angeline Lawrence

As a gift for completing "Positioned for Power," download
prayers to keep you for the next seven (7) days at
bit.ly/7daysofprayers.

To purchase the full 31-day Prayer Journal, go to
bit.ly/31daysofprayers

ABOUT THE AUTHOR

Angeline Lawrence is a minister, working mother, writing consultant, and publisher of Christ-centered content. As a former target of workplace bullying, Angeline used the traumatic experience to transform her life instead of becoming a victim. Although she was called to the ministry in 2000, God used her testimony to inspire Christian-working women to be change-agents for Christ in the market and work place. Angeline is a victor and you can read her story in the 2015 anthology, Resilience: Living Life by Design; where eleven other women who overcome obstacles in their lives shows you how to thrive in life.

Today, Angeline Lawrence is a Huffington Post contributor and the host of the Shine & Grind Podcast where she interviews leaders, entrepreneurs and experts who provide strategies to strategically overcome adversity in order to be champions in this world.

You can stay connected by subscribing to the Shine Now Magazine, a bi-monthly digital magazine that will encourage and inspire you to be the best you can be. You will discover helpful tools, tips and insights from experts who inspire women to continue to be a light in the workplace.

Angeline earned her Bachelors of Art in Economics and Masters of Urban Planning from the University of Michigan and has worked as an Urban Planner in diverse communities for over 20 years. She resides in Metro Detroit with her husband and children.

STAY CONNECTED & JOIN OUR FACEBOOK COMMUNITY

Righteous Women of Faith
bit.ly/RighteousWomenofFaith

www.ingramcontent.com/pod-product-compliance
Lightning Source LLC
Chambersburg PA
CBHW071139090426
42736CB00012B/2163